Tikanga

Tikanga

An introduction to **te ao Māori**

KERI OPAI

PHOTOGRAPHY BY
TANIA NIWA

upstart press

A catalogue record for this book is available from the
National Library of New Zealand

ISBN 978-1-990003-17-2

An Upstart Press Book
Published in 2021 by Upstart Press Ltd
26 Greenpark Road, Penrose
Auckland 1061, New Zealand

Reprinted 2021, 2022

Designed by Nick Turzynski, redinc. book design, www.redinc.co.nz
Photography by Tania Niwa, www.tanianiwa.com
Cover illustration by Ilycia Laverty
Printed by Bluestar

For Aunty Dot — almost a centenarian and still 'respectfully curious'.

Contents

Preface: te ao Māori — the Māori universe

THE MĀORI WORLD IS, in fact, a Māori universe with all of the subtleties, idiosyncrasies and nuances of any culture. In this book, we will peer into the wharenui (meeting house) with respectful curiosity and learn to appreciate some of the fascinating intricacies of the people, language and culture of indigenous Aotearoa.

Tikanga is, simply and broadly speaking, a Māori 'way of doing things': the customary system of practices and values that are expressed in every social context. Based on the root word 'tika', to be right, correct. What the appropriate thing to do is in the circumstances. It is the constant, yet flexible, gravity of the Māori universe.

While, for many years, there has been a steady anthropological attentiveness to Māori things, ways and people, in recent years the interest and appetite to learn more about te ao Māori has grown exponentially among Pākehā people, recent immigrants and Māori who are disconnected from their language and culture.

This interest is welcomed by Māori, especially as it is on a personal level, as opposed to a distanced or scientific viewpoint, and it is the reason for this book. My intent, therefore, is not to attempt to write some sort of comprehensive handbook on an entire Māori universe, but it is an endeavour to guide the beginner to te ao Māori and begin to explore some aspects of it based on and around tikanga Māori (Māori customs and protocols) and te reo Māori (Māori language). However, this brings up the first challenge for me in writing it: how to assure you that I know what I am talking about without sounding boastful or arrogant.

Māori are not a homogeneous people. Each iwi (tribal nation), hapū (sub-tribal nation) and even region has very distinct attitudes, perspectives and tikanga. I was brought up in Taranaki and educated and instructed in the ways and worldviews of my iwi/hapū/region of Taranaki, and one of the central pillars of a Taranaki ethos is to be humble. At all times. In all things. One of my elders told me: 'Whakapāpaku i a koe, hei rangatiratanga mōu' — 'To humble yourself is the attribute of the truly noble'.

Imagine how difficult it is in any job interview when your prospective new boss asks the inevitable question: 'Tell me about yourself . . .' and you have been trained to be humble and not sing your own praises!

I have found it extremely difficult to answer that seemingly innocuous question because every fibre of my being is screaming to not give a hint of arrogance lest my people find out and my mana (respect, status, pride, influence) is diminished. (Mana is an integral cog in how the Māori world works and we will explore that in the first chapter.)

One method I have employed in the past to cope with this conflict is by having an advocate to speak on my behalf. This can come across as the prospective new employee not being confident or articulate whereas, in fact, the Taranaki Māori interviewee is adhering to their tikanga, as they must, to 'bring their whole selves' to the new job. At one interview, I mumbled my way through the various questions designed to bring out information about me, my interests, experience and knowledge and, becoming frustrated with how difficult it was to skirt around the hints of being considered egotistical by my people, I ended up half throwing over my curriculum vitae and saying: 'I'll let my C.V. speak for me.'

Fortunately for me, the interviewer had been briefed on the Taranaki philosophy of humility and my reluctance to talk about myself and so the knowledge, experience and achievements articulated in my C.V. were enough to quickly sway the boss. I got the job.

But, dear readers, that still leaves us with the dilemma, doesn't it? Why should you give credence to what I say in this book? Who am I to think myself knowledgeable enough to write with any authenticity or authority about tikanga and te ao Māori?

For the sake of expediency and because having an advocate speak for me is not possible in this case, I will merely list a number of things that I have done and experienced, and then you can decide whether or not to take on board what I have to say.

I . . .

- Was trained and instructed by kaumātua and mātanga mātauranga Māori (Māori knowledge experts) from an early age. I am now in my fifties.
- Started teaching te reo and tikanga at seventeen.
- Was a kōhanga reo teacher at nineteen.
- Began teaching as a Taranaki Polytechnic tutor at twenty-one, their youngest at the time.
- Gained a Māori interpreters licence at twenty-one, the youngest licenced interpreter in Aotearoa at the time.
- Have, since then, been translating and interpreting everything from iwi Deeds of Settlement to children's books.
- Have three published children's books that I advised on and translated.
- Have taught at kōhanga reo, primary and secondary schools, kura kaupapa (Māori immersion schools), polytechnics, wānanga (Māori worldview-based universities) and university.
- Have been a speaker at seminars overseas.
- Gained a master's degree in mātauranga Māori (Māori knowledge systems).
- Wrote a 50,000-word thesis in te reo, 'E'ara te reo Māori i te reo tāmi i'o i te mana wa'ine', an analysis of whether sexism exists in Māori language or not — a unique thesis topic written in Taranaki dialect.
- Created Te Reo Hāpai — The Language of Enrichment. A te reo glossary for the mental health,

addiction and disability sectors using positive Māori worldviews, including creating terms in te reo that previously did not exist, e.g. pāmamae heke iho (intergenerational trauma), mātau ā-wheako (lived experience), takiwātanga (autism).

■ Won an award in the Mental Health Service Awards of Australia and New Zealand in recognition of contribution to excellence, innovation and best practice in mental health services, for the creation of Te Reo Hāpai.

■ Was a finalist for the Tupu-ā-Rangi Māori Television national award for science and health.

■ Launched Te Reo Hāpai as a website with audio function and new word/concept additions, e.g. Aroreretini (ADHD), Manaakiao (Williams Syndrome).

This book is aimed at locals and visitors alike, but as a point of difference, it is my intention in it to share the answers to a universal question that can elude other publications with a similar topic.

Simply, why.

There is much information on the what, how and even when concerning tikanga. But not a lot on the reasons the elements of tikanga have developed. My kaumātua (this word is both singular and plural so in this case — 'elders') would always say: 'The real wānanga is always why.' 'Wānanga' means to contemplate, to think deeply about something and is also a learning experience.

Also, as much as I know, as much as I have been taught, as

much experience as I have teaching, living and breathing the marae and te ao Māori, I have always maintained a childlike fascination with it, a deeply respectful curiosity about it and a beginner's eye and full appreciation of it and its wonders.

I hope you will join me on our journey to understand and explore more in these pages.

Chapter 1
Te reo and respect

Speaking te reo

If we follow logically the premise that words, language and how you use them have power, can something as peripheral as pronunciation of te reo Māori also have the potential to have deleterious or beneficial effects?

I believe so, yes.

You may have noticed in recent times more of an effort from the various radio and TV channels to include some phrases in te reo in their broadcasts. During the news, segues such as 'E haere ake nei' — 'Coming up' and 'Kia ū tonu mai' — 'Stay tuned' are used or during the sporting segment you may hear 'Ki te hākinakina' — 'Now to sport', 'Ki te rīki' — 'To rugby league' and a myriad of other such phrases.

This used to be more common during Māori Language Week, but these days it permeates state-run media. It may have been a commercial imperative to not continue to butcher te reo on NZ TV, but as well as this, it is just in line with a more general acceptance and encouragement that one of the official languages should be valued and respected.

Keep an eye on that word, 'respect'. To show respect is incredibly important in any culture, and for the longest time for Māori people, we haven't felt that our language has been respected. So here, in practical terms, is something that anyone can do to show respect for te ao Māori: learn to pronounce te reo Māori well. Please!

TE WHAKAHUA — PRONUNCIATION

I believe that one of the fastest ways to show respect for anyone and any culture is to learn to pronounce their language well. I don't think you need to become fluent in every language to do this, but wherever I have gone in the world I have worked on a few key phrases and local customs to show my respect for the local people and country that I am in. And that opens doors, hearts and minds tout de suite.

So, it stands to reason to first learn to pronounce the indigenous language of this country, especially considering the amount of time everyone who lives here will be saying Māori placenames.

Imagine how much more difficult it is to establish a rapport with someone when you can't pronounce their name properly (or respectfully) or if you never say their name for fear of mispronouncing it. And how would you feel if someone you interacted with on a regular basis constantly mispronounced your name (some of you may have had that experience). At the very least you would find it annoying and therefore it would be more difficult to merely establish any sort of friendly or working relationship.

For me, the formula to keep in mind is quite simple: if you show respect for the language, you are showing respect for the culture; if you show respect for the language and the culture, you are showing respect for the people.

Right, so how to avoid these sorts of uncomfortable interactions. The following is a basic guideline to pronouncing te reo well. There are also many apps and YouTube videos that can help. I recommend ones from reputable sources like Te Taura Whiri i te Reo Māori/The

Māori Language Commission. The online *Te Aka Māori Dictionary* is a useful resource that also lets you hear a word's pronunciation.

CONSONANTS

There are eight consonants:

H K M N P R T W

Most are just pronounced as in English, but the slightly tricky one is 'R'. The best way I have heard to describe its sound is as in the word 'purr'. The cat 'purrs'. If you learned to roll your 'r's when you were a child, this will come more naturally to you. If you didn't, it is harder to learn but you can do it!

Digraphs

Digraphs are two letters that make one sound. In Māori there are combined consonants:

NG = as in ring, sing
WH = as in far

Try saying 'ringer' (also a good exercise to practise the 'r', but I recommend you try one new thing at a time). Then add an 'a' — 'ringa'. Then try 'ringa', 'singa', 'blinga'.

It just takes practice.

A quick note about 'whaka' (this is called a 'causative prefix'). Yes, it sounds like the infamous swear word in English. But te reo isn't English! It isn't a swear word. Please

Pronunciation tangles

A couple of quick examples of where incorrect pronunciation has the opposite effect.

I once stopped at a gas station on my way to a tangihanga (Māori funeral — tangihanga is the full term for a 'tangi') to ask for directions to Tīrau. I asked the customer service representative for the directions while pronouncing 'Tīrau' properly (Tee-ro). Before he even answered with any advice on a route he insisted on 'correcting' my mispronunciation. 'It's Tee-row mate, Tee-row!' (with the 'ow' in 'row' said as if someone has stood on your foot). I gently informed him that I was a teacher of te reo Māori and a fluent speaker and that it was very definitely pronounced 'Tīrau'. He then doubled down and insisted that I was wrong; it had always been called 'Tee-row' and he added the epically classic line with utmost vehemence: 'Look mate, it's Tee-row. I should know, I'm a local!'

On a train once, in the Wellington station, a flustered woman who was obviously running late jumped on quickly and asked me if this was the train to 'Para-param'. In all sincerity, I turned to her and said: 'No. This is the train to Paraparaumu.'

She consequently got off and missed it.

I had no intention of being mean or misleading. I simply couldn't answer her in the affirmative because, for me, the mystical land of 'Para-param' doesn't exist. And mispronouncing Māori placenames, and Māori people's names, is the equivalent of denying the history and whakapapa (genealogical connection) contained therein.

I did feel quite sorry for the woman as the train pulled out of the station and I have often wondered if there was a way of handling the situation better. In my defence, I was a teenager at the time.

fully pronounce words or placenames that start with 'whaka'. It is 'Whakatāne', not 'Wakatāni'. First, that isn't a word and, second, again, by mispronouncing people's names or placenames you unconsciously end up denying the history and whakapapa of that person or place.

Vowels

Quick question: how many vowels are there in te reo? If you answered 'five', technically, you are correct. But I would like you to think that there are actually ten vowels in te reo because there are ten distinct vowel sounds and putting the emphasis in the wrong place can alter the meaning of the word. Don't worry. This is not as complex as it sounds. You only have to remember one rule for clarity: that while there are five vowels in te reo Māori, each one of these can be pronounced short or lengthened (the macron above the letter indicates a lengthened vowel), e.g.

**a, e, i, o, u and
ā, ē, ī, ō, ū**

If you have never had the opportunity to learn how these sound, the good thing is that most sounds in Māori language are also in English. So you have already spoken them at some stage.

The short vowel sounds are like the following:

**a = about
e = enter
i = ticket**

o = organ

u = put

For the lengthened vowels it is a case of a similar sound for a slightly longer period. Think of:

ā = far

ē = red

ī = keen

ō = door

ū = moon

Mistakes are inevitable but forgivable. And they can lead to some interesting conversations. See the following example for demonstrating how important vowel length is:

taua = **that, the aforementioned**

tāua = **you and I**

tauā = **a war party**

You probably don't want to get 'you and I' and 'war party' mixed up! Like anything else, this just takes practice. But master the basic pronunciation of te reo and 99 per cent of the time your pronunciation of new words will be right and 100 per cent of the time you will be showing respect for the language, culture and people and your efforts will be appreciated. Making mistakes is natural when learning anything new so have patience with yourself but do practise, practise, practise! Me heke te werawera! — To perspire is to be expected when you make a supreme effort!

Diphthongs

Diphthongs are two vowel sounds run together as a single syllable. The sound begins with one vowel and moves towards the other. I have added familiar sounds, words and phrases (at least, in English pronunciation in this country) to help guide pronunciation:

āe	ai	ao	au
high	bite	tower	coat

ea	ei	eo	eu
pear	lay	mentor	et tu, Brute?

ia	ie	io	iu
beer	siesta	seesaw	few

oa	oe	oi	ou
borabora	cortex	toy	doh

ua	ue	ui	uo
David Tua	tube	Louie	who saw

Other tips

Every Māori word will end in a vowel and can be divided into syllables consisting of:

a consonant plus a vowel or vowels — ka, nui
a single vowel — a
a digraph plus a vowel — ngā

Something relatively simple but that can make all the difference in Māori people perceiving the effort that non te reo speakers have made worthy of respect is the emphasis placed on a Māori word. Think of any non-native speaker of English that you have ever met. Recall their pronunciation and emphasis on parts of English words. Do they stress the right ones? Don't you feel the utmost respect for someone who was brought up to speak another language as their first language yet seems to speak English better than most native speakers? Think of the many speeches given in a forum like the UN. Isn't it admirable when people can speak a number of languages and are equally fluent in all of them? I know I am suitably impressed listening to these people. The same goes for a non-native speaker of te reo. Someone who has put the effort in and by no means is fluent or has the vocabulary of someone who was brought up speaking te reo Māori as their first language but *sounds* like a native speaker with the Māori words that they know.

Here is the secret — emphasis. Where you stress within the words.

Syllable stress

Māori language (and, in fact, most languages of the Pacific) are based on a syllabic stress rhythm. So, syllables. 'Whakatipu' is said 'wha/ka/ti/pu'. Aotearoa is 'ao/tea/roa'. Pikopiko is pi/ko/pi/ko etc.

This takes a bit of getting used to but is relatively straightforward and consistent.

Another really important secret to help with fluidity

and fluency with the Māori words that you know, might learn or say every day and want to pronounce properly is this little gem: Māori words generally emphasise the first syllable(s) of the word. So, it is <u>Ta</u>ranaki, not Tara<u>na</u>ki. It is <u>Wai</u>kato not Wai<u>ka</u>to and it is <u>Wha</u>nganui, not Wha<u>ngā</u>nui or Whanga<u>nui</u>. And by the way, it is definitely not 'Wanganui'. That word is nonsensical and doesn't mean anything.

So, when you see or hear a new Māori word or placename, try this new knowledge out. There are a few exceptions, but as a guide this works the majority of the time. Try these random words:

hauora (health), rorohiko (computer), kaiwhakaako (teacher), pukapuka (book), Tongariro (the mountain)

Keep in mind folks, these are just guidelines to helping you gain knowledge and confidence in your pronunciation in a comparatively short time. The linguistic study of te reo Māori is a fascinating but complex subject and is beyond the scope of this book. There are, of course, abundant resources for this study if you are so inclined. There are many books and university courses, but my personal recommendation is *Reo Māori o Nāianei — Modern Māori* Books 1 and 2 by P.M. Ryan. A fantastic resource with lots of practical examples. It emphasises practice over too much grammar-speak.

If that is the way that you prefer to learn, tukuna kia rere — go for it, but after teaching thousands of people over the years I have found very few who *sounded* fluent by learning only grammar. Of course, there are many ways to learn, but my interest here is the impetus on learning to pronounce te reo well in the first instance.

Keep in mind that simple equation: if you show respect for the language, you are showing respect for the culture; if you show respect for the language and the culture, you are showing respect for the people.

Just a side note. If this book seems quite laden with te reo, it is because it is difficult to separate te reo from tikanga, and it is probably folly to do so. They really go hand in hand and back each other up. Also, Māori worldviews tend to be holistic. The legendary Sir James Henare, kaumātua elder statesman of Northland and grandfather of current (in 2021) sitting Member of Parliament Peeni Henare, famously said: 'Ko te reo te mauri o te mana Māori' — 'The language is the life force of Māori mana'.

He mana tō te kupu — words have power
·······························

One of the taonga (treasures) that was taught to me was the ability to understand the ways and thinking of our tūpuna (ancestors) by analysing the construction of words in te reo, the etymology of words and the language itself. Much like the English school teacher who is the only one who knows (and is interested in) word origins, I feel very privileged that I was given this taonga. Of course, it is from my Taranaki wellsprings of knowledge so other iwi and regions will have variations in their explanations. So, I will bring these words and elucidations up as appropriate.

I'd like to start with this one: Pākehā.

Considering some of the ludicrous interpretations for this word that I have heard, I can understand why some Pākehā people may take offence at it. White flea, white pig, the list goes on (my favourite is 'Moonlight glinting off the cheek of a Pākehā person at night!').

The reality, according to my elders, is a little more down to earth but equally interesting. Similar conceptually to elsewhere in the Pacific, in Samoa — Paalangi, in Rarotonga — Papa'ā:

pā — to touch, strike or affect (in this case, affect)

ke — from kē — different or in a different way or direction

hā — breath or essence (in this case, essence)

So, a Pākehā was a person that affected the environment differently from a Māori person. 'Māori' just means natural, normal, average. Fresh water from the environment is wai Māori.

As you can see, there is nothing inherently derogatory in the word 'Pākehā'. I think it is unique and is more appropriate for white-skinned people of this country because it speaks to the presence of people other than tangata whenua (people of the land, i.e. indigenous people of Māori descent) who are here via the treaty of Waitangi — tangata tiriti (people of the Treaty).

I remember having a quiet laugh to myself when I

heard of a Pākehā person who refused to call herself a Pākehā because she didn't want to be called a Māori word. She insisted she should be called a 'Kiwi'. Another Pākehā woman pointed out to her that 'Kiwi' is a Māori word . . .

One word that is also heard frequently as an alternate but equivalent Māori word for a Pākehā person is 'Tauiwi'. I would like to advocate for this word to stand for a person in Aotearoa who is not Māori or Pākehā. The origin of this word is:

Ngā iwi kua tau mai i muri o te Māori — The peoples that have arrived here after the indigenous Māori.

Immigrants and visitors to this country, and especially those who have dark skin, to me, are 'Tauiwi'. While they may fit under the general idea of 'affecting the environment differently', the word 'Pākehā' represents the original white-skinned settlers and their descendants and is based in a Te Tiriti (Treaty) relationship.

Language is so powerful, isn't it?

Whether you decide to uplift someone's spirit or you decide to crush it instead, this is often accomplished with words.

My kaumātua told me constantly: 'He mana tō te kupu' — 'Words have power'. So, we have to be clear and diligent in how we use them. And if we don't have sufficient knowledge, this can lead to misuse and misinterpretation.

This is what has happened to the word 'Pākehā'.

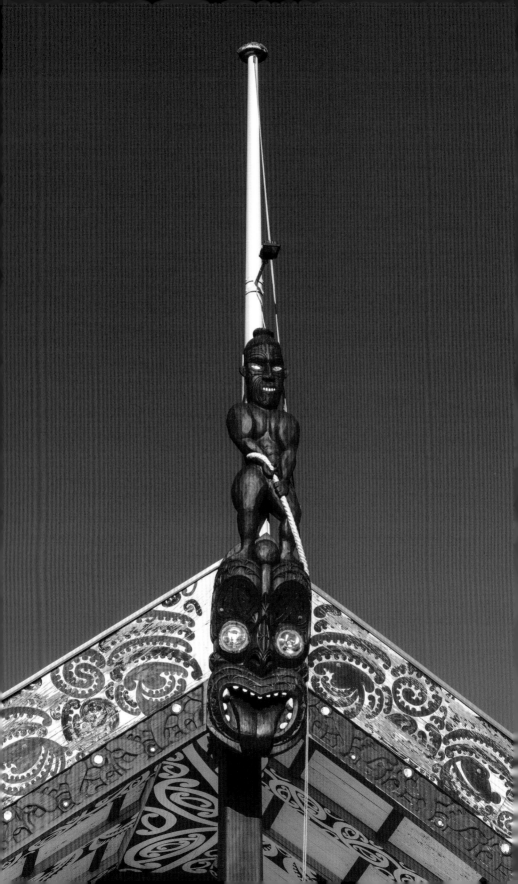

Chapter 2

Hei tāhuhu kōrero — fundamental understandings

CHAPTER 1 WAS ABOUT CREATING an opportunity for giving respect, and thereby receiving respect, in te ao Māori. It focused on using a basic working knowledge of te reo with good pronunciation, native speaker-like emphasis and other ways that make it clear you are trying to show respect, in a humble way, to the Māori language.

This chapter follows on from that progress with some fundamentals about the structures and organisational patterns of the Māori world. It is a lot easier to avoid faux pas or giving offence if you have a clearer awareness and appreciation of the ways and worldviews of Māori people, communities and culture.

Iwi, hapū and whānau

These are the fundamental structures of how Māori people identify themselves. It is not generally considered appropriate these days to use words like 'tribes' (as that can have negative connotations of primitivism), but I would call iwi, nations, and hapū communities, and these are both made up of many whānau. Keep in mind that the word 'whānau' equates to the English word 'family' but includes all members of those who are considered 'whānau'. This can be extensive and although these structures are generally based on whakapapa — genealogical and familial blood ties — others can be brought in and considered whānau based on what they have done for the whānau, hapū or iwi.

They can be adopted in, they can marry in or if they were taught by leaders of those communities that is also a relationship not necessarily based in whakapapa. Suffice to say, the word 'whānau' covers both the nuclear and extended family.

As stated beforehand, the philosophies inherent in Māori thinking and worldviews are almost always reflected in the Māori language itself so we can see mirrored in these words and concepts the relationship between people and the environment.

WHĀNAU

Whānau — pronounced phonetically 'far no' not 'far now'. And, yes, it means all aspects of family, but it also means to give birth, e.g. Kua whānau mai tana pēpe — Her baby has been born. This hints at the mana of women, whakapapa and the life cycle. Only by giving birth to new generations will the whānau, hapū and iwi survive and thrive.

HAPŪ

Hapū — a community based on whakapapa. The names of hapū often contain the name of the tupuna (ancestor) upon which the affiliation is based, e.g. Te Whānau a Takimoana or Ngāti Tāwhirikura.

Note the macron: 'hapū' not 'hāpu' as I have heard it mispronounced. A 'hāpu' in some dialects is a shop. This can be, unintentionally, quite humorous to speakers of te reo when a learner talks about giving birth to a shop! (Mistakes are a part of the process in learning anything new, so a balance must be struck between having the patience and insight to think about vocab use and sentence structure before saying something new in a learned language and also having the confidence and courage to attempt it in the first place. 'E kore te pātiki e hoki ki tōna puehu' — 'The flounder doesn't return to its disturbed hiding place in the sand'. The main thing is to learn from a mistake.)

'Hapū' also means to be pregnant. Do you see a pattern emerging with these words? Again, this dual meaning hints at the power of women, of maintaining whakapapa and the life cycle. You can't have a 'hapū' (community) without getting 'hapū' (pregnant — bringing forth new generations).

IWI

The largest conglomeration of whānau and hapū is the iwi. This word is a little more well known in Aotearoa. Again, these iwi names often contain the eponymous ancestor. 'Ngāti' is the most common introduction to the tupuna who begat the iwi, e.g. Ngāti Porou (from the ancestor Porourangi) or Ngāti Te Ata (from the ancestress Te Atairēhia). Although 'Ngāti' is the most common title before a tupuna name, there are others, including 'Te Ati' and 'Ngāi', but they mostly mean the same thing: 'The progeny of . . .'

Once again, there is a dual meaning for the word 'iwi'. As well as the title of a grouping of various hapū, it also means 'bone' or 'bones', i.e. your relatives are literally made of the same bones as you, the same blood, the same DNA, the same whakapapa. This is why you may still hear some Māori people say 'They are your bones' when pointing out kinship ties with relations. Even if the person does not speak te reo fluently, they are reflecting a Māori concept when speaking English.

WHENUA

Whenua is one more word and dual concept that I think fits in well with the above explanations. 'Whenua' means land, but it is also the word for placenta. Given the explanations above it is probably relatively easy to see the pattern here. The word for both land and placenta is the same because this recognises the connection that te whare tangata — the womb (literally the house that gives rise to people) has with mother earth — Papatūānuku. They are one and the same and people cannot survive without them. This is also reflected in the ritual of burying the placenta in the land where Māori, their whakapapa and ancestors belong. The whenua (placenta) goes back to the whenua (land). It is quite a beautiful concept and, interestingly, as part of the forming of a modern Aotearoa New Zealand, this ritual of burying the placenta has been taken up by many Pākehā in recent times.

The perpetual connection is where the concept of 'tūrangawaewae' derives. Literally, your place to stand, i.e. the place where your placenta is buried and where your ancestors lived, loved and died for a thousand years or so.

IWI DISTINCTIVENESS

If iwi of Taranaki have a tikanga or philosophy of being humble, do other iwi outside of that rohe (region) have a different way of thinking?

Yes, of course, some do.

There are certain iwi known for their forthright nature. Who stand up and speak their minds at every opportunity. Who have no problem telling others how great they are or how skilled they are at certain tasks.

I try to see this as an example of the rich tapestry of iwi variation and not judge it too harshly, but it is difficult to do so from my foundational learnings within my haukāinga (true home). Interestingly, I have heard, learnt and been taught many whakataukī (traditional Māori proverbs) that encourage humility. I haven't, as yet, found any that encourage being boastful. Being proud, yes, being bold, certainly, but none that I know of, at least, that urge egotism.

Common examples are:

- 'E kore te kūmara e kōrero mō tōna reka' — 'The kūmara does not speak of its sweetness'
- 'Waiho mā te tangata e mihi' — 'Let others sing your praises'
- 'Ko te koauau anake ka kī, ko au, ko au' — 'Only the koauau (cross-blown flute) says it is me, it is me'.

As mentioned previously, if you have little or no experience, context or a knowledge base to draw from, it is easy to clump peoples of a different culture into a homogeneous grouping where generalisations rule: 'Māori culture is so sexist', 'All the men were warriors' 'In the old days, did Māori people eat hāngī (food from an earth oven) every day?' 'Only women start the waiata (song)'.

'WE' BEFORE 'I'

It is fair to say, generally speaking, that Māori people tend to think communally, with less emphasis on individual needs and wants as opposed to what the whānau requires in order to be well or prosper. Sometimes even the hapū or possibly the iwi is paramount in some people's minds when it comes to well-being or prosperity, as opposed to the individual. This, like many philosophies in te ao Māori, is reflected in te reo and is a contributing factor as to why its system of pronouns is quite complex. It is important to define who you are talking to, who you are talking about, how many there are involved and who is being included or excluded in the conversation. Hence, 'koe' (you — one individual I am talking to), 'kōrua' (you two that I am talking to) and 'koutou' (three or more people that I am talking to).

This is why many Māori people commonly use the slang term 'youse' or a variation like 'you guys', 'you lot' or 'you fullas' (a common pronunciation of 'fellows'). In Māori thinking it often sounds wrong to use the proper English term 'you' (koe) for the plural (kōrua or koutou).

This is just the tip of the pronoun iceberg and, as you can see, it can get quite complicated. If this complexity of pronouns is quite hard, conceptually, for many learners of te reo to grasp, it is most likely because it is a uniquely Māori and Polynesian concept, as it also exists in other languages throughout the Pacific.

Atua

In explaining about whakapapa and connection to places and ancestors, it is important to spend some time discussing 'atua'. Atua are what are often referred to as 'the Māori gods'. This type of reference relegates atua to a mythical pantheon like the Greek gods, often characterised as being 'primitive' or part of 'idol worship' in the much more enlightened modern times that we live in today where we have evolved past such childlike fantasies.

Of course, this very modern world has a lot of people in it that believe in many different gods, but I will discuss ngā atua Māori.

PART OF THE NATURAL WORLD

The kaumātua who taught me were incredibly knowledgeable about atua. Like most indigenous peoples, tūpuna had such a close relationship with the natural world around them that what they could accomplish must have seemed like magic. Navigating by the stars, by winds, by sea currents over thousands of kilometres in the vast Pacific was the ancient equivalent of the moon landings. The ability to grow crops of kūmara by smelling the soil and categorising the earth into thirty distinct types, predicting the weather with accuracy in order to go fishing or gather natural resources, knowledge of gravity, of rongoā (natural medicine) and too many other amazing aspects of life to list here, allowed Polynesian ancestors to not only survive in a hostile environment but to prosper and develop into a remarkable culture and people.

Being Māori

••••••••••••••••••••••

The term 'Māori people' may be unfamiliar to some. I am using this phrase as opposed to a term like 'the Māori' because the latter term feels like it lacks the recognition of difference amongst so many of us, and it also feels like it harkens back to anthropological books written about us not by us. And who am I referring to when I use the phrase 'Māori people'? For the purposes of this book, in discussing those knowledgeable about tikanga I am speaking of those who are strong in their language and culture. Those who regularly participate in their marae, hapū or iwi activities. I am not discussing Māori folk who are disenfranchised from te ao Māori. In my experience, many Pākehā and Tauiwi are under the false impression that most Māori individuals and families are strong in their language and culture. Especially as Aotearoa as a whole is embracing more Māori language and worldviews in recent times. Unfortunately, this is simply not the case. The vast majority of Māori people and whānau Māori (Māori families), in fact, did not grow up with a strong Māori language and cultural base.

There is much data available to support this statement, but a quick relatable personal family story will sum it up succinctly.

What happened in my whānau is very typical of what happened to the vast majority of whānau Māori. My grandparents were both Māori and my grandfather, in particular, being brought up at Parihaka (a Māori community in Taranaki — there is a lot of fascinating kōrero about Parihaka so I would recommend a Google search), was the holder of te reo, whakapapa, history and Māori knowledge. When he went to school, he was beaten for speaking the only language he knew, which, of course, was te reo Māori. He had to mimi (pee) his tarau (pants) until he learnt the English words for 'May I go to the toilet, please?' This was during the time when the state thinking was that assimilating Māori people into the Pākehā or Western systems and culture was the only way forward for New Zealand. This period extended many decades, from after the New Zealand Wars or Land Wars (notice I didn't say the 'Māori Wars') from the 1860s up until the relatively recent 1960s when more and more protests started agitating for Māori rights.

Because of all the racism my grandfather experienced right from when he was a child, he (and my grandmother) decided to not bring up their kids to speak te reo Māori or to know their culture or even acknowledge their heritage. This was to enable them to have a better shot at getting on and possibly prospering in the Pākehā-dominated world. No parents want their kids to have to go through the worst aspects of their own upbringing.

So, because of this philosophy of survival at the time, not to mention out of love, my parents' generation weren't taught anything about being Māori. They were, in essence, taught to be good, very brown-skinned Pākehā.

Just contemplate the enormity of that for a moment.

You are clearly Māori. Your skin is brown. Every time you look in the mirror, the reflection is not Pākehā. But you have no awareness of what being Māori means. Your manner, appearance, behaviour and worldviews are determined by your surroundings in this Pākehā world. You strive to emulate and assimilate into a 'mainstream' society, and you are embarrassed and sometimes ashamed to be obviously Māori. This can lead to over-compensation strategies like being incredibly patriotic about being a Kiwi/New Zealander, deliberately mispronouncing words in te reo, speaking with a slight English accent to sound more noble, wealthy or educated and countless other ways of 'fitting in'.

By the time my generation came around, the connection to te ao Māori was well and truly severed for the majority.

Imagine, if you can, what it would mean if you were spirited away to, let's say, North Korea, where you could not express who you are and had to assimilate to survive.

It doesn't sound pleasant, does it? But, essentially, this is what happened and why, after generations of this ethos for survival, most Māori people are not living as Māori, and te reo Māori, as an indigenous language, is considered 'vulnerable'.

So, I mihi to you (in this context, thank) for reading this book, becoming more aware of what has happened and where Aotearoa is currently heading and making an effort to have respect and aroha for tikanga, te reo and te ao Māori. Ka rawe! (How wonderful!)

A major part of that prosperity and development was due to a relationship with atua.

So, who or what are these atua?

Keeping in mind that different iwi have different atua and concepts and beliefs about atua, I will list a few well-known ones here following the order in a karakia often quoted in Taranaki.

Ranginui = Sky
Papatūānuku = Earth
Rongo = Peace, balance
Tāne = Trees, forests, birds, insects
Tangaroa = Sea, water
Tūmatauenga = Conflict, war, anger
Haumiatiketike = Uncultivated foods
Tāwhirimātea = Winds, storms, weather

Keeping in mind iwi alternative interpretations, the word 'atua' means 'That which is beyond humans', a/tua. 'Tua' means beyond and all of these natural elements are beyond us mere mortals to control no matter the ego of some 'leaders' around the globe. You soon learn your place in the natural world when you face a hurricane or tidal wave.

WHAKAPAPA — DESCENDANTS OF THE NATURAL ELEMENTS

In terms of whakapapa, each iwi can have its slight distinctions of how people came to be in this 'world of light', but in a generic sense, a common trait is that all Māori people are descended from these elements, these atua. Some iwi have a different order to those atua born from the primordial parents, Rangi and Papa, but it is generally acknowledged that all Māori people are 'uri', descendants of the natural elements that surround us.

Of course, this is a commonly held belief among many indigenous people around the world. It helps to survive and prosper if you are part of the land, sky and sea. How much more seriously would all people around the world take environmental impacts if the earth was literally the Earth Mother from which we all sprang? If dirtying rivers meant disrespecting your ancestor and if you could trace your genealogy from the very sky and the earth right down to yourself?

So, is this just tree-hugging environmental studies gone overboard? Well, no. While science reflects prior indigenous knowledge, it is clear that humans are made up of the same elements as the stars, galaxies, sun and earth. If you and I could somehow fly up into space and scope out 'star stuff' and the particles that comprise the universe, we would find that we are made up of the same things. Oxygen, hydrogen, carbon, nitrogen. Oxygen, that is Tāwhirimātea. Humans are around sixty per cent water, oxygen and hydrogen. That is Tangaroa. These human origins gave rise to the whakataukī:

Ko wai au?
Ko te wai au
Ko te hau ahau e

(Who am I?
I am the water
I am the wind)

This is why the 'whakapono' or belief in atua Māori is not one of faith; it is merely fact. No one is asked to believe in something that may or may not exist. You can quite easily see and interact with atua at any time. Tangaroa is the sea. Not a half-naked god-man standing by the ocean with his taiaha/trident. Tāne is the forest, Tāne is the tree, not an abs-shredded warrior posing by a waterfall. When we perform karakia before cutting down a tree or we give the first caught fish back, we are showing respect for something greater than ourselves and acknowledging our place in the natural environment. We are, quite literally, part and parcel of the environment, not placed here to rule it and bend it to our will. We are part of the life cycle, just passing through:

Ngaro te kai
Ngaro te tangata ki te pō

(Just as food decomposes
So do humans provide nourishment to the
natural cycle of life)

CHRISTIANITY VS TRADITIONAL MĀORI BELIEFS

The philosophy of atua, living and breathing as part of the natural environment, has, for many iwi, been replaced by Te Atua: the concept of the Christian God. This has been a rather large bone of contention among some iwi for many years.

I was recently involved with an iwi from outside of

Taranaki who were having conflict within themselves about which path to follow and develop. In essence, the taiohi (youth, young people) were taking the kaumātua to task over the fact that the iwi as a whole was Christian based. All of their spiritual practices utilised Christian faith-based prayers in te reo, whereas the young people wanted to explore and ostensibly 'get back to' a pre-colonisation belief system of atua Māori. Eventually, a compromise was reached where the kaumātua essentially accepted that the young people were going to explore the path to atua and, in return, the youth of the iwi accepted that their kaumātua were brought up with their own belief systems and they weren't going to change at this stage of their lives.

Many iwi have either gone through this exploration of values, are going through it or will go through it. It is a fundamental principle for many. If Māori are the indigenous people of this land of the long white cloud, shouldn't we uphold and practise our traditional beliefs? And it is not just Aotearoa that is experiencing this shift in belief systems. While I was in Tahiti a few years ago, I went to one of the traditional gathering places of all Polynesians, Taputapuatea on the island of Ra'iatea. I was very fortunate to meet a 'tahua' there (the Tahitian equivalent of a tohunga, a spiritual expert). I spoke with him for an hour before he finally accepted that I, too, was tangata whenua, an indigenous person. He was petrified that I was secretly with the gendarmes of Tahiti because I was asking about the traditional tikanga and spiritual practices of the Tahitians and he knew that if I was working for them, if he confessed that the local tangata whenua still practised some of their 'heathen' ways in acknowledging the local atua, he could be hauled off to jail! So much for the freedom of belief in Tahiti! After building up enough trust, we talked for another few hours before my flight back to the main island.

Although we don't generally have to worry in Aotearoa about the police hauling us off to jail for traditional belief systems or practices, it is uncomfortable in Māori settings to practise pre-colonisation tikanga and karakia among iwi who are mainly Christian faith based. I have had to walk this balance between wanting to adhere to what I was taught with not wanting to offend or anger elders or other iwi who don't practise these traditions. As a taiohi, when I was asked to do karakia, if I believed reciting the traditional karakia would cause offence I would try to avoid it, but inevitably there were times when I couldn't avoid it and I would sometimes get a telling off for not reciting Christian 'inoi' like a benediction or The Lord's Prayer. But I simply couldn't disrespect what I was taught and what I whole-heartedly believed in. Like the kaumātua who taught me, I have always actively promoted karakia tūturu (pre-colonisation karakia) as a way for many Māori people to indigenise their thinking and reconnect with atua and the natural world that not only surrounds them but of which they are inextricably a part.

TRADITIONAL KARAKIA 'WHAKATAKA TE HAU'

A great example of a traditional karakia that many people, including Pākehā and Tauiwi, can relate to is one known as 'Whakataka te hau'. It can be seen online and has been published in many books over the years. While it doesn't name specific atua, the connection to the natural world is clearly evident and it is an excellent exemplar of the philosophy behind karakia Māori and behind atua Māori.

Whakataka te hau ki te uru
Whakataka te hau ki te tonga
Kia mākinakina ki uta
Kia mātaratara ki tai
Kia hī ake ana te atakura
He tio, he huka, he hauhū
Tihei mauriora!

(Cease the winds of the west
Cease the winds of the south
Let bracing breezes flow over the land
Let bracing breezes flow over the sea
Let the red-tipped dawn come with sharpened air
A touch of frost
And the promise of a glorious day
Let us celebrate life!)

Inevitably, there are variations on the translation and origins of this karakia, but this is how it was taught and explained to me by my kaumātua of Taranaki.

It is aspirational. The hope and desire are that the winds

of Tāwhirimātea from the west and south will die down. This places the origin of the karakia squarely on the west of Aotearoa as the winds from both the west and the south often bring inclement weather to these regions. It then goes on to refer to 'bracing breezes' flowing over land and sea. The words 'mākinakina' and 'mātaratara' are poetic versions of the root words 'kina' and 'tara', to be spiny, spiky, as in the cold, bristly wind that pricks at your skin. These are all indications of a frosty but fine morning. The red dawn is the final sign that though it may be bracingly cold, it is most likely to be a lovely sunny day.

But hold on, I thought the saying was the opposite of that. 'Red sky in the morning, shepherd's warning. Red sky at night, shepherd's delight.' This is where the Māori connection with our atua like Rangi, Papa and Tāwhirimātea is on display. Not every time, but the vast majority of the time, the conditions depicted in 'Whakataka te hau' hold true. If there is a red dawn and it is bitterly cold in the morning, generally this is an indication of a beautiful day ahead, particularly in the west of Aotearoa. The ancient saying 'Red sky in the morning, shepherd's warning' (and the American equivalent 'sailor's warning') originates in the northern hemisphere and perhaps doesn't often apply.

I named my first mokopuna (grandchild) 'Atakura' after this indicator of a wonderful fine day. Driving down to attend her birth in the early morning to welcome her into the world with karakia tūturu, a brilliant red dawn occurred and I knew that this particularly special day would be a superb one. And every day that I get to spend with her is a superb day. That is why the old people called a magnificent fine day 'He rā mokopuna' — 'A day for grandchildren'. It is a day for the older and, hopefully, wiser to spend with their grandchildren, playing with them with a child's heart, enthusiasm and zest for life, while guiding them, giving them the benefit of years of experience and the aroha that only a grandparent can bestow.

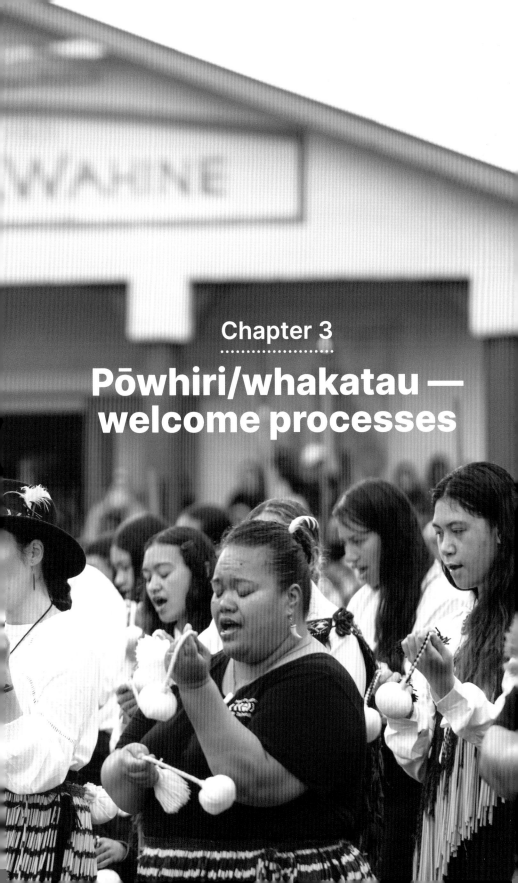

Chapter 3

Pōwhiri/whakatau — welcome processes

Variations of tikanga

At the end of my teens I was a kaiako at a kōhanga reo ('language nest') in Whanganui. As mentioned earlier, kaiako is a teacher, derived from the word 'ako' which means to both teach and to learn. This hints at the reciprocal nature of teaching and a philosophy of a lifelong commitment to learning and being curious about the world. As the whakataukī states: 'Kāore he mutunga o tēnei mea, te ako' — 'There is no such thing as an ending to learning'.

I made many long-standing relationships there in Whanganui, including time with knowledgeable people and elders, so it will always have a place in my heart. There is a close relationship between Taranaki and Whanganui and our dialectal variation of the 'h' replaced with a glottal stop is cherished and brings us closer together.

During a tangihanga (Māori funeral) on a marae up the Whanganui River, we waited for the manuhiri (guests) to arrive. Eventually they did, and after the traditional exchange of calls of welcome and response delivered by the kuia (female elders), everyone sat down to await the speeches (see the more detailed explanation of the pōwhiri process below).

A couple of minutes ticked by while speakers gathered themselves and prepared to speak. Nothing unusual about that. Then another few minutes, and another. Eventually ten minutes had passed with no one standing to speak. This was very unusual. What had happened? Why wasn't anyone saying anything? Finally, after these ten agonising minutes of silence, confusion and apprehension, the elders on the local Whanganui side indicated with a hand gesture for the manuhiri to start the speeches. And amidst uncertainty and unease, the first speaker stood to deliver his speech of farewell.

The long delay had been a lesson for the manuhiri. In Whanganui there is a tikanga, a protocol, called, unsurprisingly, tikanga Whanganui. This tikanga is unique in my experience. It is that in Whanganui, at a tangihanga, the manuhiri speak first. The lesson had been that the manuhiri had not 'done their homework' and found out what the tikanga was in this part of the Māori world. The guest speakers had been waiting for the local speakers to stand up and speak first as is the common custom among most iwi. The local elders in full cognisance of the guests' confusion had just waited patiently for them to start, eventually putting them out of their misery by indicating for the manuhiri to start the procedures.

I guarantee that no one of the manuhiri guest party ever made that mistake again.

The point of me recalling that experience to you is to emphasise that fact that Māori people, hapū, iwi and even Māori organisations are not homogeneous. There is no one size fits all. Of course, there are some shared principles and values like manaakitanga (to look after, tend, foster, extend hospitality) and aroha (love, compassion, sympathy, empathy), but it is important to be aware that there are many variations of tikanga throughout the motu (nation). What is clearly understood and normal in one region may be totally different in another. There are even variations among iwi, hapū and sometimes whānau. So, always keep in mind that 'one size fits one' while I go through aspects of the pōwhiri (welcome) process below but also while you read this book and especially in your interactions with te ao Māori.

Hui, mihi and whakatau

There are many types of hui or gatherings in te ao Māori. Most, but certainly not all, are staged at a marae. There are different types of marae throughout all of Polynesia, but in Aotearoa this is generally a complex comprising a number of buildings. Most frequently, a wharenui (literally 'large house' for gathering), a wharekai ('food house' for dining), toilets, showers and other buildings. The word 'marae' is actually referring to the courtyard immediately located outside the wharenui, but in modern times the whole complex is called the marae.

This important set of buildings and courtyard is the central focus for many iwi, hapū and whānau as it is a common gathering place that usually unites people by whakapapa, although some urban marae have been established around city centres for many Māori people too.

Hui held at marae include social events, formal welcomes, funerals and many others. Some have been adapted from Pākehā concepts like birthdays and twenty-first birthdays, while others have been retained from traditional times, such as new house openings and tangihanga. But whatever the event, if it is Māori, it will almost certainly contain a mihi, a process of greeting and acknowledging people there. At the lesser end of the formality scale, someone will stand up and greet everyone and perhaps acknowledge certain special guests or people who have travelled from afar. This is generally done by a male, though this depends on circumstances, and it is generally done in te reo or at least partly in te reo depending on the knowledge and fluency of the speaker and that of the audience. This type of mihi is very common and is becoming more and more common in the workplace and at the likes of board meetings.

A step up in formality that is also becoming more commonplace at work is the whakatau. One interpretation of this word is 'to put at ease' and the purpose of this process is to do just that. To put the person or people acknowledged at ease by welcoming them into a new work space, or perhaps welcoming new students into a school, for instance. The whakatau is yet another adaptation of a Māori welcoming process that is gaining traction among non-Māori organisations and workplaces in the ever-growing popularity of shaping an Aotearoa New Zealand identity that attempts to support Māori worldviews and practices.

WHAKATAU VS PŌWHIRI

One of the most asked questions I have fielded over the years is: what is the difference between a whakatau and a pōwhiri? The answer is that they are both processes of welcome, but the whakatau is generally less formal and not as lengthy as the pōwhiri. A typical whakatau will have some elements of the pōwhiri but not all. It will usually include a mihi but may not include some of the more formal elements most often performed by elders, such as karanga (traditional call), the whaikōrero (traditional speech) or the waiata tawhito (traditional ancient song). Of course, this all depends on the commitment of the workplace and management in employing, hiring or contracting kaumātua or exponents of te ao Māori. Some work environments see absolute alignment with their core businesses. This is particularly the case in the health sector, but it is a steadily growing outlook with many businesses and companies not customarily associated with Māori points of view.

From a te ao Māori standpoint, because of so much tokenism in the past, there can be a lot of scepticism at some of these attempts to incorporate Māori processes and perspectives. And, realistically, some workplaces, businesses and organisations have done the bare minimum to look diversified, inclusive or 'browned up', but I have been lucky to experience real commitment as well as the tick-box exercises.

Those organisations and workplaces with a genuine commitment to te ao Māori will often employ or contract kaumātua or experts in te reo and tikanga to embed language and cultural practices in the workplace as part of an attempt to be responsive to the Treaty of Waitangi or engage better with te ao Māori, especially when the clientele is predominately Māori. Yes, because it makes good business sense but also, sometimes, just because the upper management realises that it is the right thing to do.

Hui at workplace or on marae

Whether a pōwhiri (or pōhiri in some dialects) is given in the workplace or on the marae, the process and order of actions is commonly the same. The only difference is that anything Māori that has been adapted for a business or organisation is still restricted by the constraints of the employer and workplace. How many people can fit in the boardroom or meeting space? Do participants need to RSVP for accurate catering numbers? Does the schedule fit with enabling management to attend? What time limits are in play? This is always the tension with utilising Māori ways of thinking, doing and being in a work environment.

There is always a compromise because, on the marae, in a purely Māori space, these compromises mostly don't exist and would be seen as a blight on the mana of the marae. Yes, it is handy to know approximately how many manuhiri are going to arrive so that there is enough food for everyone. But as long as there is plenty of kai (food) to show manaakitanga, that's the main thing.

Yes, a six-hour pōwhiri is a long haul, but I have been to many because time is seen as being secondary to the kaupapa (the purpose or business at hand). And, having a long pōwhiri can add to the mana of the purpose of the hui. Pākehā tend to call this 'Māori time' because it can be fluid and change and is a guideline not set in stone, but really it is the tikanga, the way of being that is putting the kaupapa or people first and not having to vacate the room at 10.15 am because there is another meeting scheduled for that time. It is probably more accurate to call it 'non-Pākehā time' because this tends to be a common tikanga for other peoples in other countries, especially around the Pacific. I have travelled to many islands around the Pacific and inevitably you find the locals referring to time as 'island time' or 'Rarotonga time' and the like.

THE GENERAL PROCESS: WEAVING PEOPLE TOGETHER

For the pōwhiri process itself, let's say a hui has been called and the manuhiri have arrived. Of course, there is a ton of preparation that has gone on beforehand to get to this point, but we are focusing on the tikanga of the pōwhiri itself. And remember the story about the manuhiri in Whanganui that assumed the tikanga of the pōwhiri would be the same as they were used to? There will be regional variations, so we are just exploring a generalised version.

Again, there will be other explanations as to the etymology of the word 'pōwhiri', but it was explained to me as: 'pō' — night, 'whiri' — to weave together. So, the concept of a 'pōwhiri' is to weave the tangata whenua and the manuhiri together both in terms of time shared under the one roof of the wharenui (nights in the meeting house) and the weaving of the tūpuna, the ancestors who have gone to the great night together as well. This concept is supported by the fact that the full word for guest/visitor is 'manuwhiri' (manuwhiri/manuhiri are dialect variations). Manu — bird, whiri — to weave together. The guests are likened to birds landing on the marae for a short time, interwoven into the local tangata whenua for the duration of the hui and then they return to their homes at the conclusion.

WERO

The tangata whenua are ready, as are the manuhiri. Occasionally, this is when the challenger goes out wielding a taiaha (staff weapon). In some pōwhiri there may be more than one challenger. This wero (challenge) is relatively rare, though, and mainly reserved for greeting dignitaries or for special occasions.

KARANGA

The majority of pōwhiri start with the 'karanga', the traditional call of the women. The word 'karanga' derives from 'raranga'; again, it is the concept of weaving together the tangata whenua and the manuhiri and weaving together the ancestors and dearly departed that are carried in the hearts and minds of the participants.

The karanga is an essential part of the formal pōwhiri so may be omitted in less formal practices like whakatau. It is performed exclusively by women and generally by female elders. A well-delivered karanga can send shivers up your spine and bring a tear to your eye as well as convey messages of welcome, history and remembrance.

MOVING ONTO THE MARAE

The kaikaranga (callers) on both sides will exchange karanga back and forth as the manuhiri walk slowly towards the tangata whenua.

This ritual has its traditional roots in ancient times

and has evolved from a time when there was a process to go through to establish the purpose of the gathering and whether there was any potential for conflict. The pōwhiri is sometimes referred to as the 'ritual of encounter'. This is also why the pōwhiri starts at a distance and slowly the two parties close the physical gap.

During the ascent onto the marae, it is common for the manuhiri to stop for a short period to remember those that have passed on.

Eventually, either the time will feel right or another call will be given to signal for the manuhiri to take their place on the paepae (speakers' bench) and on the seats behind. This is assuming the pōwhiri is taking place outside on the marae ātea (the courtyard) which is the most common practice, but there are variations that I will touch on later. Generally, only men sit in the front row of seats. This is an optic that is criticised by some non-Māori as being sexist. I must admit that I find it hard to grasp that people with little to no cultural knowledge or insight can find it perfectly acceptable to negatively comment on this. I have little to no knowledge of surgery so I don't feel in a position to criticise how a surgeon holds a scalpel. There are valid reasons for the continuance of these traditional gender roles, rooted in tikanga, which are explored later in Chapter 8.

The two sides prepare to speak. Most commonly, only men speak on the marae during a pōwhiri, but there are exceptions and there are areas where women speak as well. As this is the 101 version of the basics, we will stick with what is most ubiquitous.

WHAIKŌRERO AND WAIATA

The formal speechmaking or whaikōrero begins (see Chapter 4 for explanations regarding whaikōrero). Ninety-nine per cent of the time, the tangata whenua will begin (note the beginning of this chapter for an example of when this isn't the case).

A good whaikōrero can capture your heart and mind and cement you in place in awe at the oratory expertise. It is full of historical references, traditional sayings and chants, genealogy, witticisms, humour and the heartfelt. At its best it is a pleasure and a privilege to experience.

Each kaikōrero (speaker) will stand, give a speech in te reo and conclude with a waiata. A waiata is a song. But it is not just a random selection. It must complement the whaikōrero and support it. If an inappropriate waiata is performed, it can be devastating. It may indicate that the singers of the song do not agree with the speaker or that they are ignorant of what the speaker has talked about. There is a lot of mana and power present in the waiata.

The word waiata means this: wai — water, ata — reflection so, the wai-ata is a reflection of what the speaker has talked about or it is a reflection of the kaupapa of the hui. As a quick example, I once gave a whaikōrero and people rushed up to sing my waiata. While I appreciated the gesture, the waiata was not well chosen and was the equivalent of a nursery rhyme to support my long-thought-out and complex speech. I turned and thanked my supporters and then quickly turned back to the manuhiri and performed a more traditional and appropriate waiata by myself. Not long afterwards a respected kuia on the manuhiri side thanked me for adhering to tikanga. She said: 'Kātahi te moumou kōrero!' — 'What a waste of a good speech that nursery rhyme was!'

ORDER OF SPEAKING

At this juncture of the pōwhiri it is important to mention the two main kawa or procedural rituals. The most common is 'pāeke', which is the tikanga where the tangata whenua all speak first and then hand it over to the manuhiri to speak. You can see the origins of the 'ritual of encounter' in the name of this kawa, 'pā' — fortified village, 'eke' to ascend onto the pā, perhaps in conflict.

The other main kawa used principally by the various iwi that descend from the waka (canoe) of Tainui (from South Auckland down to the Mōkau River) and the iwi who descend from the Te Arawa waka (from Maketū in the Bay of Plenty area to the Tongariro district) is known as 'tū atu, tū mai' or 'tauutuutu' and a few other variations of the name. The first name is the most descriptive and makes the procedure clear: 'tū atu' — the tangata whenua stands first, and then 'tū mai' — the manuhiri stand and speak. This alternates back and forth until all the speakers have had their say, but the tangata whenua always stand last and conclude this process.

The word 'whaikōrero' literally means to 'whai' — chase, pursue, the 'kōrero' — the speeches including the topics and/or the challenges. This is the art of oratory. The thrust and parry of the sharp witted. As mentioned, I will discuss this more in the next chapter, but it is worth saying at this stage that with the decline in native speakers of te reo and the relatively low number of engaging eloquent whaikōrero artists that practise today, I long for the days of yesteryear when your ears hung on every word of the true whaikōrero master.

BECOMING ONE — HONGI AND KAI

Whether the kawa be pāeke or tū atu, tū mai, eventually this essential part of the pōwhiri comes to an end. Usually this is when a koha from the manuhiri is placed on the ground not far from the speakers of the tangata whenua. A koha is a gift or a contribution of money. In general, it is to aid with the costs of the hui. In traditional times it would have been kai or a taonga, a treasured heirloom or cherished possession. When this is laid down and received by the tangata whenua, they will indicate that the rituals have been fulfilled and it is time to be one together. This is accomplished with the hongi. The pressing of noses. Note that it is the pressing of noses, not rubbing noses. Different iwi have differing explanations as to how this has come about but suffice to say that it is the Māori personal greeting that breaks down the last barriers of the possibility of conflict by being in close proximity with each other and sharing breathing space.

Once again, different iwi have slight variations of the hongi, whether it is two presses of the nose or one, whether foreheads should touch, whether there is a handshake or an embrace of the shoulders, or whether the women are kissing on the cheek. Hongi is the traditional greeting while kissing is a modern variation so while in the line awaiting the hongi, I recommend looking ahead so you have an idea of what to expect. Some iwi have staunchly encouraged their hapū and iwi members to stick to the hongi and not to kiss. I once heard one stalwart of traditional tikanga say loudly so that everyone could hear: 'Whakarongo ki te pakepakē mai o ngā ngutu pāua!' — 'Listen to the smack smacking of all the pāua lips!' She was not pleased.

Once the hongi is over, generally, kai is then provided and everyone goes to the wharekai (dining house) to partake in food together.

RATIONALE FOR THE PŌWHIRI PROCESS

The above are the common practices and the conventional order of actions — the what. But why? Why are these things done? And why in this order?

One of my kaumātua would always say: 'The real wānanga is always in the why' (wānanga in this context is fascination, depth and learning opportunity).

If you think back to the original 'why' for the pōwhiri, as mentioned, it is the ritual of encounter; it has come from a time when it was unclear why two distinct groups were meeting, perhaps for the first time. It was a time when there was uncertainty about a group approaching. What was the purpose? Was there potential for conflict? Through a series of actions the purpose of the meeting was established and even in modern times when it is very rare to have much in the way of physical conflict, the fact that for most iwi the pōwhiri takes place outside on the marae ātea, the marae forecourt, the place of potential conflict (full name — te marae ātea a Tūmatauenga, the courtyard of the god of war, anger and conflict) is clearly stating that if there is conflict (mostly verbal disagreement these days) outside is the right place to verbally spar, not in the wharenui which is considered to be the place of Rongo (the god of peace).

EXCEPTIONS TO THE RULE

There are exceptions to this but, again, this is the general, most common scenario played out on marae all across the nation, every day.

One of the main exceptions to this generalised pōwhiri procedure is when, for whatever reason, the tangata whenua change the tikanga of the day and have the pōwhiri inside. This could be due to many reasons, but it is often just being practical. When it is incredibly stormy outside, for instance. I have seen some marae decide to have the pōwhiri inside the wharenui because it was so cold outside it could endanger the health of the manuhiri and especially the kaumātua. In this example, the tangata whenua decided that the ultimate way to manaaki or look after their guests was to change what they would normally do so that the well-being of the visitors was of paramount importance.

The same basic order of actions would remain; however, they would just be done inside the house.

The second exception is an interesting one. Some iwi and hapū just have a different way of doing things. I have seen manuhiri karanga first. Very unusual, but it has happened. I have seen kuia speak on the marae. Pretty rare, but it does happen. I have seen the wero go very wrong and there has been a physical fight on the marae. Again, it is extremely rare, but it does happen occasionally. The pōwhiri is not just a ceremony that people have to get through in order to get to the biscuits in the wharekai. It has to be taken seriously because you never know if it will be one of the exceptions that prove the rule. I have been around for a while and seen and experienced some of these things, but they are extremely uncommon. It is unlikely that if you are Pākehā or Tauiwi reading this book that you will experience these situations.

However, one example of difference in the tikanga of the pōwhiri that you have a higher likelihood of experiencing is the kawa of Taranaki.

Once again, let me emphasise that there are variations but, in general, in the Taranaki region the vast majority of pōwhiri are conducted inside the wharenui. The approach to the marae ātea and wharenui is the same, but when the manuhiri get close to the house they proceed inside. This can be quite disorienting for those that have never encountered this tikanga before. Then the next big surprise: the hongi is first, not last. After the hongi the manuhiri go and sit down and the rest of the procedures are very much the same as described above. There are a couple of other tikanga that are unique to Taranaki if the manuhiri are from within Taranaki itself, but suffice to say that this illustrates clearly that not all Māori people, hapū and iwi exhibit a homogeneous worldview. In fact, it is better when talking about a Māori worldview to use the plural: Māori worldviews.

Tapu and noa

If the real wānanga is in the why, what is this all about? Why can't people just turn up to any marae and walk into the wharekai and help themselves to a cup of tea? Yes, I've talked about this ritual coming from pre-colonisation times, when there was the possibility of conflict, but what is the deeper philosophy at play here?

An ethos that permeates the Māori world is that of the concepts of 'tapu' and 'noa'. That which is tapu (restricted, prohibited, sacred) and that which is noa (free from tapu). All of the actions and protocols of the pōwhiri are ways and means of lifting and clearing the tapu of the visitors. The karanga, the calling from afar, the whaikōrero, speechmaking — these traditional rituals establish the reason for the hui. You work out any potential for conflict, talk it out, establish peaceful intentions and then you proceed. There is no hongi without this being fulfilled. There is no going to the wharekai to break bread with one another if some 'take' (issue) between the two groups has not been worked out. Eating kai together is another means of lifting tapu. As is the hongi. Even the waiata is part of the kawa of lifting tapu. There are some iwi and people who maintain that the waiata is just 'kīnaki' (relish) for the whaikōrero. My elders were very clear about the role of the waiata: 'Hei hiki i te tapu o te whaikōrero' — it is to lift the tapu of the whaikōrero. The speeches inevitably include farewells to the dead, perhaps whakapapa, ancient chants and karakia, the words and sayings of tūpuna — all tapu things. As mentioned before, the waiata has much power. You can infer many things, put a point across and agree or disagree employing the right waiata. Wai/ata — you look in the water and see the reflection.

All of these things ritually contribute to the lifting of the tapu of the manuhiri, clearing the way for the hui ahead. We will be delving more into tapu and noa in following chapters.

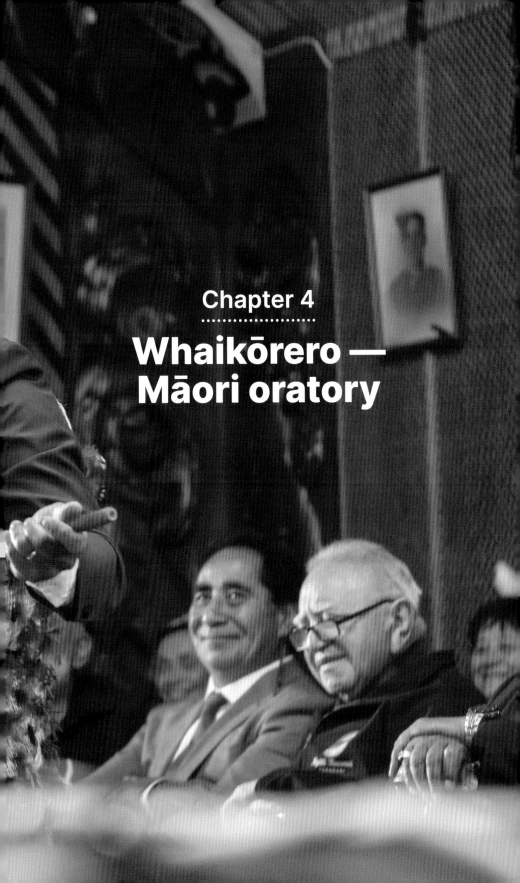

Chapter 4

Whaikōrero — Māori oratory

THERE IS A QUALITY in the art of Māori oratory that is hard to explain. This applies in many other languages, I expect. It is the equal of any Shakespearean sonnet or soliloquy, rife with metaphor, comparison, inference and nuance that only whaikōrero aficionados can truly understand and appreciate. For a people who depended on an oral history and narrative transference for 800 years, it is the epitome of knowledge and wisdom. Good whaikōrero can fix the attention for hours on end.

My first whaikōrero was when I was seventeen. There were no other men on the marae at the time and manuhiri had turned up out of the blue. No warning, they were just there. My tauheke (Aotea region dialect word for male elder) turned to me and said: 'Well, it's only us. You've got thirty seconds to think of something to say . . .'

Not unsurprisingly, I was incredibly nervous. I had never spoken formally before on the marae. What would I say?

Yet somehow when I stood to speak, I knew instinctively what to say. I could remember, word perfect, the right chants and proverbs to use and the right phrases to make people feel welcome. Although my kōrero was relatively simple in comparison to later times as my knowledge grew, it was clear, moderately eloquent for a first timer, especially as a teenager, and it drew supportive comments from the manuhiri like 'Kōrero!' (Keep speaking!) and 'Tautoko!' (We support what you are saying!)

I don't know how exactly I had the words and the chants to use. I can only surmise that I had been around such acclaimed, knowledgeable speakers that, through osmosis, I had picked up everything I needed to know and, thankfully, could retain it and reproduce it.

I'll never forget the look on the face of my tauheke. It was a mixture of disbelief, quiet pride and puzzlement, as in 'where did that come from?!' That was the first of only three times in thirty-five years when he complimented me. 'Ka pai, e tama,' he said. 'Well done, boy.'

Having done a few whaikōrero since then, let's journey through some typical common guidelines as to what is said and why.

This is, of course, pitched at a basic level for the readers of this book. If you are truly interested in exploring the art of whaikōrero further, I recommend a marvellous book by Dr Poia Rewi, *Whaikōrero: the world of Māori oratory*. It is based on his doctoral thesis written in te reo Māori, which is also stunning.

The art of discussion

Let us explore more of what I touched on in the previous chapter with the composition of the word in te reo for a speech or speechmaking — 'whaikōrero'. It is a combination of 'whai', to chase, to pursue, and 'kōrero' — speak, discuss, discourse. So, to 'whaikōrero' is literally to 'whai i te kōrero' — 'to chase the talk'. What that means is that the essence of whaikōrero is kōrero, it is discussion, it is talking with wisdom about a topic. Yes, the whaikōrero is certainly enhanced by eloquent phrases, various chants and proverbial sayings, but essentially, it is the art of discussion, of debate.

Usually, someone will bring up a 'take', a topic for discussion or debate. The various speakers after him should either add to the topic, discuss it more or bring up their own issue to discuss. It could be anything, really, but my favourite topic is when kaumātua raise a historical issue between the tangata whenua and the manuhiri. Each side has its version of events and issues to sort out. And time has no meaning here. It could be from a year ago or a hundred and fifty years ago. The depth of knowledge that is brought to bear is captivating. You have to bring out the right traditional chants and sayings, quotes and songs. It is a fantastic sight to behold and treat to listen to seeing and hearing the old people undertake these vehement discussions on the marae.

Sometimes they become so animated for a short time they behave like young men again with 'kaioraora' (songs of derision) and haka performed with the vibrancy of men fifty plus years younger. I have no doubt that they are aching for days afterwards, but it is truly magnificent to see the old people perform these traditional chants and movements.

Nature of the language

Again, I have to put in a bit of a disclaimer here. I'm about to run through things that my elders (male and female) taught me. How other areas learn and perform whaikōrero might be different, but I think there are some widely accepted 'norms' that we will explore.

Like the fact that, for the most part, the type of language

Kaumātua

• • • • • • • • • • • • • • • • • •

You will see that I use the phrase 'the old people' a lot. This can sound derogatory. It is, in fact, complimentary. As discussed, in Māori worldviews getting older and becoming an elder is something to be respected as your knowledge and, hopefully, wisdom matures with age, even if the body isn't quite what it used to be. So, to observe 'the old people', males and females, performing some of these ancient chants and recitations is a rare treasure.

I once saw a staunchly authentic group of elders strip completely naked to perform a manawawera (an impassioned type of haka without uniformed actions). Later, I asked them why they did this. Their reply was that their tūpuna didn't wear Pākehā clothes when they performed this manawawera hundreds of years ago, so to honour their original ancestors they felt they needed to be true to the time and memory of that performance. Ka mau te wehi! — Now, that's impressive! And, luckily, it was a warm day . . .

We'll discuss kaumātua again in Chapter 9.

used is formal and eloquent. It is not the normal, collo-quial, 'pass the salt' conversation, full of slang, you might have at the dinner table. For the most part. I did once see a man come out and speak on the marae who had, moments ago, been stirring the pots in the kitchen. He was dressed as he should for that job, in gumboots, shorts and a singlet, but he displayed a knowledge of history, mixed perfectly with both poignant and hilarious kōrero, full of jargon from his dialect and slang terms that only a gifted native speaker of Māori could deliver. He wowed us with a great, entertaining whaikōrero that, while not fancy or eloquent, was one of the best examples of whaikōrero I have ever heard. As soon as his waiata was over he turned and walked back into the kitchen to continue stirring the pots and cooking our kai. It was almost surreal.

For many years in some regions and within some iwi, there has been a dearth of speakers of te reo who speak Māori as their first language. What this means for the art of whaikōrero in these areas is that they have had to cope however they could. This has meant that some people speaking on the paepae have learnt, by rote, entire speeches in te reo and they just change them according to the kaupapa.

I remember as a teen sharing the paepae with a man in his fifties. He got up and delivered a well-crafted whaikōrero with poise and vehemence, and I thought to myself, 'Wow, he is a real gun at this.' Unfortunately, by the time he had spoken for the third time that day, I was literally mouthing the words of his whaikōrero as he said it because it was the same whaikōrero over and over again. It was disappointing, but I don't blame the man. It wasn't his fault that he couldn't actually speak Māori and he was just doing his best to uphold the mana of the paepae in the way he knew how.

That was how some kaumātua taught their tauira (students). The philosophy was akin to 'learn this while I am alive and can answer your questions and teach you and after I'm gone you can learn to speak te reo'.

Regrettably, this didn't really happen and most students that were taught this way didn't go on to learn to speak in te reo. Unless you are brought up speaking Māori or you have several years in which you don't have to work to earn a living to dedicate to the pursuit of learning to speak fluently, it is an incredibly difficult goal to achieve. Unlike French, Spanish or English, there is almost nowhere you can just decide to go and live where te reo is spoken fluently around you twenty-four seven. I so hope that won't always be the case.

Whaikōrero process

WHAKAARAARA

For the actual order of different parts of the whaikōrero, to begin there is usually a 'whakaaraara', a cry of alert or introductory exclamation. This gets everyone's attention, introduces you and clears the way for you to speak by letting everyone know that you are about to launch into your whaikōrero. There are variations, of course, but the most common is 'Tihei mauriora!' — 'the life principle sneezes!' Yeah . . . it doesn't translate well, does it? I explain its origin and context below.

TAUPARAPARA

After the whakaaraara, usually what follows is known as a 'tauparapara'. Because the whaikōrero has evolved from the 'ritual of encounter' and its inherent uncertainty of the purpose of the hui that we explored in the previous

'Tihei mauriora'

Tihei (and its variations 'tihe', 'tihewa' and others) means to sneeze. Mauri is life principle and ora is to be alive/healthy. Whole books could be written just on the concept of 'mauri', but the essence of this unique Māori concept is as a celebratory utterance; it is to celebrate life and its wonders. The expression has come from the pūrākau (iwi narrative) that explains the whakapapa of how human beings came into the world. Keeping in mind there are iwi variations and that this is a very truncated version, the atua, Tāne Mahuta, asked the earth mother, Papatūānuku, how he could bring humans into the world. She told him to form a woman out of the earth at her pubic region called Kurawaka and to breathe life into this newly formed female being (this is also one of the explanations for where the hongi has its origin). He did so and the being called Hineahuone (literally 'the female element that comes from the soil') awakened alive. She consequently sneezed and the phrase 'tihei mauriora' was born.

chapter, the origin of the tauparapara is as a type of traditional protective karakia that are chanted at the beginning of the whaikōrero. This has the explicit purpose of shielding the speaker from any ill will in the form of charms or curses that may be wielded against him, hence the term 'tauparapara' — kia *tau* ngā *parapara* — for any *ill will* to *fall*. While that particular circumstance may be pretty rare in contemporary times, these rituals come from a time when mana, tapu and noa ruled the world and a kaikōrero took a risk if he spoke out of turn or brought up an issue that he knew wouldn't go down well with the listening audience. Certainly, battles have risen out of both deliberate and accidental insult. Hence, this whakataukī:

'Kaua te ware e tū ki te marae' — 'Let not the ignorant stand to speak upon the marae'

In pre-colonisation Aotearoa, you certainly never saw (or heard) people who were not qualified to speak formally on the marae. They represented their iwi or hapū so they were very skilled orators. These days, because of the scarcity of experts of traditional oratory, the paepae has opened up to many more people of various degrees of skill, including some who, in my opinion, shouldn't be attempting whaikōrero until they are much more accomplished and practised. The idea is to practise at home, in your own area first so that you can be corrected by your own elders/ teachers before you might make a mistake representing your people outside of your area and perhaps bring a loss of mana to them. As the whakataukī states:

'Tangata akona ki te kāinga, tū ana ki te marae, tau ana' — 'When the person trained at home stands to speak on the marae, they are confident and at ease'

This might seem harsh, and while it is unlikely any battles will happen because of a perceived insult, some iwi take this very seriously. To the outside world, it can seem as if these rituals of challenge, expressive gestures and dramatic performances are all for show, but most encounters that happen on the marae are real and are certainly not for the tourist trade. While physical fights are extremely rare, much more common is a loose derogatory remark that leaves a blight on someone's mana and that can lead to years of the 'parapara' or ill will lingering around like a bad smell. Like the Māori tendency to prefer dealing face to face with people, word of mouth reigns supreme in te ao Māori.

'Tangata takahi manuhiri, he marae puehu' — 'A person who insults or mistreats their guest has a dusty marae'

In other words, the marae will merely gather dust because the people won't come back.

Perhaps this is why my kaumātua was so pleased with my first attempt at whaikōrero. While I hadn't been particularly trained in it, he recognised in my teenage self the potential to gain a good understanding of the nuanced world of whaikōrero that I had entered into. And that could only be a helpful addition to te reo, te ao Māori and particularly for Taranaki who had very few kaikōrero left at this time.

Traditional tauparapara are, quite simply, wondrous. They speak of history, whakapapa, tūpuna, they are full of symbolic language, allusions, metaphor and analogy, they contain traditional vocabulary that is otherwise never heard and, most importantly, they contain the worldviews of traditional times. This is often rare to find in modern times so a good whaikōrero artist will have a vast repertoire of these at his disposal.

The tauparapara should match the kaupapa of the hui or hint at what the speaker is going to talk about. For instance, if a whaikōrero is given at a tangihanga, there are specific tauparapara that refer to loss and aroha or compare death to reptiles that stalk you and natural phenomena like lightning and earthquakes. There are many that refer to the importance of learning if the kaupapa is perhaps education, or what health is in Māori thinking if that is the topic to be discussed in the hui.

A good rendition of a tauparapara is a treat to listen to, and you will observe many people closing their eyes to focus their attention on the beat of the chant and the metaphoric language contained therein. He rawe! — They are marvellous!

Obviously, whole books could be written just on the subject of tauparapara, so, for the sake of expediency, here are a couple of simple examples. For a general hui you might hear:

Ka tangi te tītiī
Ka tangi te kākā
Ka tangi hoki ahau
Tihei mauriora!

(The muttonbird calls
The kākā [parrot] cries out

As I exclaim
Tihei mauriora!)

Tauparapara and indeed, in my opinion, whaikōrero in general should be left to the experts. There are plenty of other opportunities for discussion in which everyone can participate. This is a traditional role and should be left to those skilled in it.

Here is another example frequently used at a tangihanga for a male elder who has passed away:

Te tai rā, te tai rā!
Te tai rā e pari ana ki whea?
E pari ana ki te kauheke, kaumātua
He tipua! He atua!

(Life's tidal ebb and flow
Where does it flow to now?
It flows to the old fellow
He who has become one with our ancestors,
and the elements!)

These examples are relatively common and have been published many times, but to me, they are still treasures and are tapu. Very special. Sacred. Like karakia tūturu they were not handed out lightly to all and sundry. These days, though, I see them and others that are much longer, deeper and some that no doubt belong to certain iwi available on YouTube and on social media platforms. I'm realistic; I know the people that put them up are only trying to help the learning process, and to share in their enthusiasm, but I was taught many of these things only by the traditional methods of listening and repeating, by deep wānanga (contemplation) over the meaning and the slow, gradual process of comprehending over years of experience. That, to me, is authenticity. Learning off YouTube feels like a fast-food version. It isn't good for you.

MIHI

Next, if the speaker is part of the tangata whenua, there would be a brief mihi to the manuhiri:

> **Piki mai, kake mai, haere mai ki te marae e tau nei — Welcome, ascend upon the marae that lays settled before you**

If the speaker is from the manuhiri, there might be a brief mihi to the local people:

> **Tēnā koutou katoa e whakatau mai nei i tēnei taiopenga — Greetings to you all, those who have so graciously welcomed this group of guests**

The manuhiri will then turn to greeting the house and marae. The manuhiri should always mihi to the whare and the marae. Like the local tangata whenua, the meeting house and the marae are providing the manaakitanga, the shelter from the elements, and they are part of the local people's ancestry. The whare often represents an ancestor so it is important to mihi to them with phrases like:

Te whare e tū nei, tēnā koe — The house that
stands before us, I greet you
Te marae e takoto nei, tēnā koe — And the marae
that lays before us, I also greet you

Like any mihi phrases, they can become quite elaborate.
Again, any good speaker will have numerous phrases like
this up his sleeve:

Te pātaka o te kupu kōrero a ngā mātua, e tū, e tū,
e tū — The storehouse of the sacred words and
knowledge of our ancestors, stand, stand strong

Te marae kua mākūkū nei i te roimata, i te hūpē,
takoto mai, takoto mai — The sacred marae
moistened by the tears and mucus spilt in sorrow,
lay there, lay before us

In recent years, I have experienced a change in the focus
of the mihi to the whare and marae. Now, I hear more
and more some speakers from the tangata whenua
greeting their own whare and marae. I don't believe this
is appropriate. As the saying goes:

'Waiho mā te tangata e mihi' — 'Let others sing
your praises'

EXTENDED MIHI

The next part can be an elongated mihi to the tangata
whenua/manuhiri. It is fantastic to hear wonderfully

metaphoric phrases to pay homage to guests or the locals. You would usually start with those with traditional roles (kaikaranga/kaikōrero) and kaumātua and work towards the workers who have put the hui together.

A few examples include:

Tēnā koutou e kui mā, e koro mā — Greetings to you, learned elders

Tēnā koutou e ngā puna roimata, e ngā puna mātauranga — Greetings to you, the wellsprings of tears, the wellsprings of knowledge

Tēnā koutou e ngā ringaringa me ngā waewae o te marae — Greetings to the very hands and feet that enabled our marae to function today

Tēnā koutou e ngā ringa huti punga — Greetings to the mighty hands that can lift the anchor stone

And a note here: because the true whaikōrero is considered tapu, it would be unusual to hear any mention of kai during the pōwhiri. Thanking the cooks, for instance, is usually left for after the hui, with delightful phrases like:

Tēnā koutou e ngā ringa wera, e ngā rae wera — Greetings and thanks to you of the burnt hand and sweat-ridden brow

A major part of most whaikōrero is the farewell to the

'mate', the deceased. Tūpuna from long ago, and the deaths of those who have more recently passed away, can be a major component of any whaikōrero.

E ngā mate o te rā, o te wiki, o te marama, o te tau, haere, haere — The dearly departed of the day, the week, the month and of the year, farewell

It is here that real poetry can be heard.

Haere e ngā mate huhua, haere ki te kāpunipunitanga o te wairua — Farewell to our many departed, go to the gathering of spirits

Haere ki te huihuinga o te kahikatea, haere ki te huihuinga o te kahikatoa — Go to the assemblage of the great trees, the white pine and the red mānuka

Haere ki tua i te pae o maumahara — Go beyond the horizon of remembrance

Tūpuna and the mate are so revered that it feels disrespectful to farewell them with anything but the most poetic of phrases. Of course, this comes down to the skill of the orator, but most speakers on the paepae will do their best to come up with a plethora of elegant phrases in order to venerate the mate.

From here the focus may settle again on the tangata whenua/manuhiri, thanking them for running the hui or turning up in person, especially if groups have travelled from afar. This recognition of the effort it takes to coordinate and physically get a group, especially a large group, to a hui or tangi is echoed often in the karanga:

Haere mai e ngā manuhiri tuarangi e — Welcome visitors who have come from beyond the distant horizon

As previously mentioned, in the Māori world, there is great mana in being there in person and expressing thoughts face to face. I was recently speaking on behalf of the tangata whenua at a tangi. A group turned up who had travelled for over eight hours to be there in terrible weather that became almost flood conditions. I lavished mihi and mana upon them in gratitude for this feat:

Ahakoa te haka mai a Tāwhirimātea, kua tae ā-tinana mai koutou! Ka tere kitea te ngākau ū tonu o te Māori tūturu — Even though the weather god, Tāwhirimātea, is engaged in his ferocious haka, you have braved the elements to be here in person! One soon recognises the rare commodity of the genuine Māori heart and its courage

KAUPAPA

The last part of the bulk of the whaikōrero is usually the kaupapa. What is the hui all about? What is the purpose? If the hui is a tangi, clearly, the kaupapa is the tūpāpaku (the deceased present), but if not, the kaupapa is teased out, discussed or even debated here.

E mihi ana ki te kaupapa nāna nei tātou i whakakotahi ake i te rā nei — I acknowledge the purpose of this hui, that which has brought us together and unified us this day

Here is the 'kōrero' part of the whaikōrero and it is quite often the part that is disappointing to my ears. This part requires being able to speak fluently and not just have mihi phrases, chants, whakataukī and other rote-learned expressions.

This 'section' requires knowledge, opinion, contemplation, the ability to debate, challenge, or come up with something new to add or something interesting to say. This requires experience and often training under a kaumātua. The best way to prepare for this, and for whaikōrero in general, is to be taken under the wing of a learned elder and serve a type of apprenticeship. This can last decades but it certainly prepares you well and is why I maintain it is best to leave the peak of language use and knowledge to experienced, witty, charismatic speakers.

As I mentioned at the beginning of this chapter, there are some iwi and rohe that don't have the luxury of being able to leave whaikōrero artistry to the knowledgeable and the trained. Some places, whānau and marae are lucky if they have one or two speakers and often these people have to cover a number of marae in their areas.

Until many more Māori are brought up speaking te reo as their first language, this will often be the case.

WAIATA

An appropriate waiata is usually chosen at this stage. It is sung by the speaker and supporting group or whānau and sometimes the speaker will just sit down at the end of that or they may say a few words in conclusion of their kōrero.

It is pertinent to remind you at this stage that the most common type of whaikōrero that I have run through here is just a template. An accomplished speaker can cover all of these topics and more in any order that he so chooses because of his knowledge, oratory skills and vast experience in speaking formally. It also depends on the kaupapa of the hui, who the audience is and any number of contributing factors that can change the pattern of speech on the day.

But I tell you, there is nothing quite so wonderful and satisfying than when you can listen to and appreciate a kaikōrero with the combination of experience, eloquent language, clever turns of phrase, a deep knowledge of history and a boundless depth of thought. Te mutunga kē mai o te pai — it is the pinnacle of excellence.

'Kōrerorero te manu tūī. Ko te kereru, ngunguru kau ana' — **'The tūī has a vocal range to be coveted whereas the bush pigeon merely coos'**

Pākehā and whaikōrero

Do Pākehā have a place when it comes to whaikōrero? While Māori debate whether Māori women should whaikōrero or not, my opinion remains that this is a traditional role whose burden and honour should only be given to the matatau (very knowledgeable), just as, I believe, only Māori women and kuia should perform the sacred duty of karanga. I admire those few Pākehā men I have met that are very fluent in te reo and who believe their place is to support iwi/hapū/whānau/marae in ways other than having speaking rights.

However, I feel there is one exception to this rule of thumb. At a recent tangi where I was on the paepae as tangata whenua, a small group of only Pākehā arrived. They had clearly worked with the deceased person for many years and admired, respected and even, for some, loved the man to whom they wished to pay their respects. We welcomed them as usual with karanga and whaikōrero and wondered what they would do when it was their turn to speak.

Usually, with solely Pākehā groups, it is understood that they might not have access to someone to speak in te reo on their behalf so we would conclude the formal ceremony by lifting the tapu on English, thus allowing them to speak, or they would not speak at all and simply hongi and greet the whānau pani (bereaved family) to show their support. Instead of this, one of the Pākehā men stood up, visibly shaking with nervousness, and stumbled through the few Māori words he knew with well-practised pronunciation. 'Tēnā koutou,' he said. 'Ka nui te aroha, nō reira, tēnā koutou, tēnā koutou, tēnā koutou katoa.' And he sat down. In English this means: 'Greetings to you. We have great sympathy, empathy and compassion for you. In conclusion, I greet you all.'

After the formalities were over, I stood up and spoke in English, which is very rare for me to do at hui and tangi. I wanted the Pākehā manuhiri to know how much I appreciated them coming to the marae and struggling through an experience that was quite difficult for them but, out of loyalty for the man they had known and compassion for his family, they felt a duty to adhere to Māori protocol and not revert to English but instead struggle to speak the few words of te reo that they knew.

That act was based upon aroha, and, to me, was quite courageous — and worthy of respect.

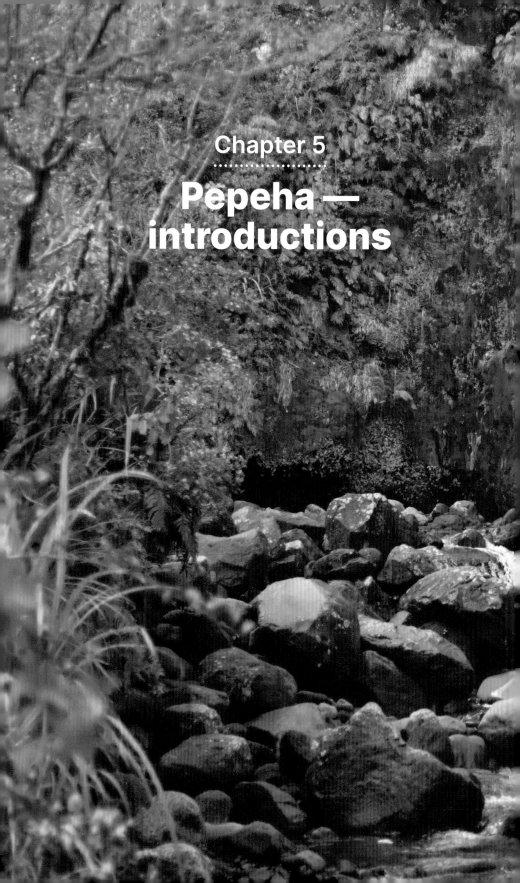

Chapter 5

Pepeha — introductions

Making connections

The pepeha or 'Māori introduction' is a staple in the life of Māori who are immersed in te ao Māori. It is also becoming an essential part of 'the new norm' in the life, and especially the work life, of Pākehā and Tauiwi. It is a familiar template of phrases that defines and describes iwi/hapū/whānau for Māori folk but also associations, backgrounds and whakapapa for non-Māori.

This is a uniquely Māori concept of introducing oneself and derives from a situation at any hui where people would stand up and introduce themselves so that those present would be able to place them among the vast lines of whakapapa of that iwi, hapū or marae. The person introducing themselves would typically mention their whakapapa affiliations via their ancestral mountain, river, waka, iwi, hapū, marae and other kinship ties, while the kaumātua would talk among themselves and place the person being introduced with phrases like 'that's so and so's boy' and 'that's my moko' (moko — short for mokopuna).

In essence, it is an introduction for any person and their affiliations in a Māori context for one purpose, to *make connections*. I'm emphasising this because most people mistakenly think that the pepeha is all about introducing yourself. Yes, of course, that is part of it, but hopefully, by this stage of the book, you are noticing patterns in Māori thinking, and one of those patterns is to not be self-centred or self-absorbed. The whānau, hapū, iwi and even rohe generally takes precedence over oneself.

The pepeha has developed out of a need, in an ever-expanding world, to connect with others of the same iwi/hapū/whānau or rohe, especially for those who weren't brought up within their kinship groups. For many Māori people who are not strongly connected to te ao Māori, this is one of the mechanisms to reconnect with those kinships and to feel a sense of belonging. This desire to feel part of a collective, to know one's place in the larger scheme of things and to have a real sense of belonging and a confidence in that belonging, is also a reason that the pepeha is very popular with many businesses, organisations and Pākehā and Tauiwi. This is especially the case in courses on te reo Māori, tikanga and te ao Māori.

THE PEPEHA MODEL

Many institutions teach the pepeha model with little to no variation; whether you are Māori or not, the template to follow is the same. I think there are three main reasons for this. First, as previously mentioned, most people think this is all about introductions, whereas it is in fact mainly about making connections. Second, not many people know the origins of the pepeha and consequently why the template is in the order that it is (see below). Third, there is an uncomfortable truth about sharing or teaching the pepeha structure. Some Māori people believe that this is only for Māori themselves and is, therefore, inappropriate for non-Māori to say. I believe that it is appropriate for non-Māori to have and use a pepeha but that when you understand the reasoning and tikanga behind it, the pepeha for non-

Māori is structured differently from that of a Māori person, making it appropriate for Pākehā and Tauiwi.

It is important at this juncture to say that having the most basic pepeha memorised and pronounced well is an admirable goal and will get you through if this is required.

Pepeha structure

GREETINGS

The structure is simple. Always start with a greeting and end with a greeting. Say your name and where you are from.

> **Tēnā koutou katoa — (Greetings to you all)**
> **Ko . . . . . . au — (I am . . . . . . [name])**
> **Nō . . . . . . au — (I am from . . . . . .)**
> **Kia ora tātou katoa**

Start with a more formal greeting like 'Tēnā koutou katoa' and conclude with a slightly more familiar one such as 'Kia ora tātou katoa.' Don't be too complex in explaining where you are from. Remember, even at this basic level, this is mainly about making possible connections. Unlike Māori people (at least, those who know their iwi/hapū/whānau/region affiliations), this question for Pākehā is often overthought into a spiralling maelstrom of confusion. Does it refer to where I was born? Or where I grew up? Or where I live now or where I spent the most time? The answer to the question 'Where am I from?' for the purpose of this most basic pepeha is simply where you believe you are from.

It could be in answer to any of the questions above, but keep in mind that you are trying to make connections. Who is the audience? Are they local Māori folk who would like to know that you grew up not far from where you are speaking or that you were born in the local hospital perhaps?

Pronunciation

As always, good pronunciation is the key. I once heard a government minister (who shall remain nameless) speak at a Māori event. She stumbled through a few jumbled, mispronounced words in te reo to start her speech. When she finished, she was challenged as to why, with all her resources, she had not prepared properly to address a Māori audience with some tuition on pronunciation. Her reply to that challenge was that she was speaking in her Pākehā dialect.

Yeah, nah. That's not a thing. There is no such thing as a Pākehā dialect. There is good pronunciation and bad pronunciation. Hers was the latter. This reply also went down with the Māori people listening like a lead balloon and the result was jeering from the audience.

So, practise, practise, practise. Good pronunciation is, at least, part of the key to great engagement with te ao Māori.

Now, let's examine the typical structure of the Māori pepeha and its origins in order to determine just what is appropriate for whom.

Tēnā koutou katoa
Ko ...... te maunga
Ko ...... te awa
Ko ...... te waka
Ko ...... te iwi
Ko ...... te hapū
Ko ...... te marae
Ko ...... rāua ko ...... ōku mātua
Ko ...... au
Tēnā tātou katoa

Translated that is:

Tēnā koutou katoa — Greetings to you all

Whenever someone stands to speak or address an audience, they will (or, at least, should) start with a greeting like this.

Ko ...... te maunga
(Name) is my mountain

Even though the definitive is 'te', 'my' is implicit here.

Ko ...... te awa/moana
(Name) is my river/large lake/body of water

Ko . . . . . . te waka
(Name) is my ancestral canoe

See below for more explanations regarding the position of the waka in the pepeha.

Ko . . . . . . te iwi
(Name) is my people/nation/tribe

As discussed in Chapter 2, the word 'tribe' isn't considered appropriate to use these days as it can imply 'primitive', but I include it here because at this time it is still used quite commonly among Māori as an English equivalent for 'iwi'.

Ko . . . . . . te hapū
(Name) is my smaller, more closely related people/nation/tribe

Ko . . . . . . te marae
(Name) is my marae

Ko . . . . . . rāua ko . . . . . . ōku mātua
My parents are . . . . . . and . . . . . .

There are many variations to the pepeha and this part stating parents or guardians may not be necessary, say, if a whānau is well-known. It may be more appropriate, for instance, to say that they were brought up by their grandparents or they were fostered by others in their hapū.

The point is that pepeha is about making connections and not always just about relations by blood.

And finally:

Ko ...... au
I am (name)

Order of pepeha

Notice the order of the pepeha. The name of the person who is identifying themselves is absolutely last and this is always so. Simply because the person who is speaking is a direct result of their ancestry, their whakapapa, their history. They could not exist without all of these things. This is the indigenous truth. And it is both humbling and empowering.

I haven't spent much time with Māori people in gangs and in prison, but I have spent some time with them. Most of them didn't know much if anything about their whakapapa, history, pepeha or relationships with iwi, hapū and whānau, and many seemed like they were looking for these sorts of connections. It is much harder to lose yourself if you are connected to your environment and to so many other relations. There is power and mana in knowing one's self and a humble pride in embracing relationships with whanaunga (relatives).

VARIATIONS

Some of the variations include where the waka is positioned in the pepeha. This is often down to regional differences. In Waikato, there is a greater emphasis on the one waka of that region, Tainui, that unites the iwi there, so often the pepeha will start with that. In Taranaki, there is no one main waka that is quoted in pepeha commonly; there are three — Tokomaru, Kurahaupō and Aotea, so there is not quite so much emphasis on these. The dominant feature that unites all iwi of Taranaki is the mountain Taranaki itself so if the waka is present in the pepeha it is usually positioned straight after the awa, not as the beginning statement. Again, the idea is to start with the wider affiliations, narrowing down to the speaker.

Another variation is perhaps famous tūpuna. If the waka is quoted, this is frequently followed by the famous captain of that waka.

Ko Tainui te waka, ko Hoturoa te tangata (Tainui is the ancestral canoe, Hoturoa is its captain), ko Aotea te waka, ko Turi te tangata (Aotea is the waka, Turi is the captain)

THE WATER CYCLE

The pepeha itself can get quite complex with the tūpuna and whakapapa lines of descent quoted or details of the names of various whare of the marae or many other differences, but there is a reason Māori follow this pattern.

Once again, this is knowledge from the whare wānanga, the traditional house of learning, that I am sharing because it informs the decision about whether the pepeha for Māori people should be exactly the same for the non-Māori population or not. And it is this: the pepeha follows the pattern of maunga, then awa/moana, iwi, hapū, marae because it is following the water cycle. As indigenous people we are part and parcel of the environment, especially the water cycle. 'Mau', as in the word 'maunga', means to catch, capture, hold. The maunga catches and holds the snow, sleet, hail and rain which eventually forms rivers and lakes, the water of which nourishes the people and which inevitably evaporates and returns to the sky and the cycle begins again.

The pepeha is indigenous code for: Māori people are part of the natural environment and water cycle. That is why the term for fresh water is 'wai māori'. And that is why the word for 'who' in te reo is 'wai'. Most people in classes learning te reo are taught the phrase 'Ko wai koe?' (Who are you?) or 'Ko wai tō ingoa?' (What/who is your name?) Actually, these phrases are far too blunt. The old people were more likely to use the phrase 'Nā wai koe?' 'Who do you belong to?' But, literally, 'From whose waters do you descend?'

This is why I believe that it is inappropriate for non-Māori people to use the same pepeha as tangata whenua. It is not a matter of mere opinion, of like or dislike, of right or wrong: it simply doesn't make sense. It is a matter of indigeneity. The Māori language has evolved over a thousand years or so to literally encode indigeneity in its composition. The pepeha is a reflection of this, even if the cypher to this puzzle has been lost to the majority of people in contemporary times.

Pepeha for non-Māori

You may be thinking to yourself: this is good and all but what about me (if you are not Māori)? Where do I fit in? Do I have a pepeha?

Fear not, dear reader. Keeping in mind that the pepeha is much more about connections and creating the potential for connections, I have created a pepeha for non-Māori based on a similar template, but with more appropriate information and phrasing. This template satisfies the needs of making possible connections with people in the audience but does so without misappropriating any indigenous ties to land, water and air. The potential here is that if listeners want to explore those connections, they will most likely approach you afterwards to discuss the details about yourself that you have given.

Also, remember to commit to memory the most basic form of pepeha first — ko (name) au, nō (place) au — in case you have to say this without any preparation or you may be nervous and decide to just stick with the small version.

When delivered with good pronunciation, I have seen this work wonders with a Māori audience many times. Respect is given and received, and it almost always has people coming up to the speaker wanting to compliment their pronunciation and discuss the details within their pepeha. Here is the template:

Tēnā koutou katoa
Ko Ingarangi
te whakapaparanga mai
(engari)
Ko ......te whenua tupu
Ko ......te kāinga
Nō ......au
Kei ......au e noho ana
He ......au i ......
Ko ......au
Tēnā tātou katoa

This may seem like a lot to try to learn off by heart, but keep in mind that this is a 'pick and mix' scenario. You don't have to include everything, especially when trying this for the first time, but rather pick what you think might be relevant for the audience and what may generate some interest in possible connections or relationships.

Let's go through it:

1.   Tēnā koutou katoa

As always, start with a greeting. There are many different ones and it is good to have a variety for different occasions. As a general rule, start more formally: tēnā koutou, tēnā tātou etc.

2. **Ko Ingarangi — England/English**
3. **te whakapaparanga mai — is my ancestry**

This could be as well as, or instead of, 'Ko Kōtirana' (Scotland/Scottish), 'Ko Aerana' (Ireland/Irish), 'Ko Wēra' (Wales), 'Ko Tairana' (Thailand) or anywhere from around the world. Pick as many as you affiliate to and can pronounce well. Often Māori are interested in the ancestry of non-Māori friends, whānau and colleagues because they consider it important whakapapa or sometimes because they have ancestry there themselves. This is a ripe opportunity to make a connection. I have ancestors from Killarney in Ireland and Valverde Del Majano in Spain so I'm always keen to hear if anyone has affiliation to these places.

4. **engari — but, however**

It's not required, although if you are confident and your pronunciation is sound, ka pai, go for it!

5. **Ko . . . . . . te whenua tupu — (placename) is where I grew up**

Another great opportunity to create an association. Perhaps someone in the audience grew up in the same place or near to it. Perhaps you both went to the same store or school. By stating the place where you grew up, you are making possible connections without misappropriating the ancestral mana of a landmark like a mountain or river. If you grew up overseas, this might also be seen as interesting, exotic or there may be a whakapapa link as in number 3.

6. Ko ...... te kāinga — (Place) is my home

Where do you call home? No matter their ancestry or where someone grew up, most people have a place they consider home. Another chance to forge a link.

7. Nō ...... au — I'm from (place)

Although these statements can all sound similar, there are subtle differences. I have heard many Pākehā and Tauiwi offer a different answer to all of these. Remember, it is pick and mix. If the answer is the same for two or more, you do not need to say the same thing several times.

8. Kei ...... au e noho ana — I am living in (place)

How many times have you told someone where you live and they make a remark based on their experience of the same place: 'Oh, what a beautiful city', 'Oh, the traffic there is terrible' etc.

9. He ...... au i ...... — I am a (job title) at (name of work/organisation)

Again, this is contextual so may not be necessary, but often people like to know what you do to seek some common talking points. Perhaps a hapū is looking for a researcher at the moment or maybe someone in the iwi has something to trade for some work in the weekends fixing up the marae etc. It is best if you can discover a term in te reo for your job, but these can be hard to find or the job title may be too specific to be in a Māori dictionary, so if you think this may be important, say the title in English.

Like the hongi which is close, face to face and breaks down personal barriers, these statements are designed to give non-Māori people a chance to bond with listeners who are Māori over commonalities that have the potential to bring people closer.

10. Ko . . . . . . au — I am (name)

Once again, there are some variations here. You can just say your first name if you are known to the audience or put your full name in if you think it might offer a chance at connection. You could also replace this with 'Ko . . . . . . taku ingoa' — 'My name is . . . . . .'

11. Tēnā tātou katoa — Greetings to one and all

Always bookend with greetings.

Occasions for pepeha

On the marae the most common time to hear people reciting their pepeha is perhaps in the evening after karakia in a whakawhanaunga session (whakawhanaunga — literally 'to make relations' so to explain people's relationships with each other). In workplaces that have adopted tikanga Māori it can be similar as it may be during a whakawhanaunga session, but generally, of course, this is in work time. Perhaps there has just been a whakatau or a pōwhiri. Perhaps a new staff member has just been welcomed into their new job. A whakawhanaunga session gives staff members an opportunity to welcome the new worker and to say who they are in relation to them.

This session is usually conducted in English or, at least, conducted bilingually as the whakatau or pōwhiri is most likely to have taken place completely in te reo. And, if that is the case, it is likely to have only included male speakers. It therefore opens up the floor to anyone to speak, including the new staff member's manager. It also often affords the opportunity to the members of the manuhiri who brought the new worker in to farewell them or for whānau members to talk about the person. This is a nice introduction to the new worker and can bring closure to their ex-colleagues, especially if it is an abrupt departure or the staff member is particularly well liked.

A common theme that is expressed in these exchanges is the promise that if the new colleague is not looked after properly by the new workplace, the ex-colleagues or whānau who brought them will come back to return them to their former job. It is usually played off as amusing and the standard reply is that the new co-workers and bosses will, indeed, extend their manaakitanga to the recently arrived new staff.

One last interesting detail about this form of pepeha. Sometimes, instead of the definitive 'te' being used as in 'Ko Taranaki te maunga', the possessive 'tōku' may be used as in 'Ko Taranaki tōku maunga' — 'Taranaki is my mountain'. Many kaumātua have shared with me the fact that they don't like this use of 'tōku' because it can imply the speaker is saying that the mountain (or other feature) belongs exclusively to them. This would, no doubt, be by accident, as no one would believe that a mountain or river belongs exclusively to them as opposed to the hapū/iwi, but it is still commonly preferred that people use the 'te' form.

Other examples of pepeha

While the above is the most common form of the pepeha, as mentioned, strictly speaking, any saying with an identifying landmark falls under the general term 'pepeha'. If a saying has a particular mountain, river, iwi, hapū, ancestor or any identifying feature that is part of a local tangata whenua area it is a type of pepeha. Here are some common and famous examples:

'Ko Waikato taniwha rau. He piko, he taniwha, he piko, he taniwha'
'Waikato River of the multitudes of taniwha

(fabled monster). At every bend there is another taniwha'

This is a reference to the many rangatira (leaders, chiefs) who came from and lived in the Waikato region. And why the famous Waikato rugby team is not coincidentally called 'The Chiefs'.

'Te Arawa māngai nui'
Literally, 'Te Arawa of the big mouth'

This is why interpretation should be left up to the well-informed. It is actually a reference to the witty and talented speakers on the paepae who have descended from the iwi and hapū of the Te Arawa waka.

'Ko Hikurangi te maunga
Ko Waiapu te awa
Ko Porourangi te tangata
Ko Ngāti Porou te iwi'

'Hikurangi (on the East Coast) is the mountain
Waiapu is the river
Porourangi is the eponymous ancestor
Ngāti Porou is the iwi'

This is an example of the basic template above but including the main ancestor who begat the iwi Ngāti Porou.

'Ngā tukemata o Kahungunu'
'The eyebrows of Kahungunu'

A reference to the attractiveness of the eponymous tupuna of the third largest iwi in Aotearoa, Ngāti Kahungunu. He was also a hard worker so if you put these two features together you can understand why he had nine wives. The attractiveness is said to be a trait handed down from him to his many descendants.

'Te Atiawa te toki tē tangatanga i te rā'
'Te Atiawa is an adze that cannot be loosened by the rays of the sun'

There are at least a couple of interpretations of this pepeha, but this is the one that I subscribe to: it is a reference to the unity of the Northern Taranaki iwi of Te Atiawa. The iwi is likened to an adze, an incredibly important tool in traditional times and depending on its status and the material used, sometimes a symbol of mana and leadership. The two main parts are the mata (blade head) and the kakau (handle). The inference is that no matter the amount of time that the metaphorical adze (Te Atiawa) laid out in the heat and rays of the sun, the bindings holding the head of the adze to the handle would never loosen. So it was with the strength in unity that Te Atiawa enjoyed in pre-colonisation times.

These are just a few examples of this type of pepeha. There are literally hundreds of pepeha that are peculiar to iwi and hapū around the motu and an expert in whaikōrero and karanga will likely have many stored in their memories to bring out at the right moment. It can be a great compliment to have a visiting dignitary use a pepeha that pertains to a particular iwi or hapū as opposed to a generic whakataukī. Some of these less well known pepeha can be quite obscure so if a kaikōrero or kaikaranga uses them in their formal whaikōrero or karanga it shows their experience and knowledge and affords them great mana.

Chapter 6

Tangihanga — the Māori funeral

The importance of death

It is quite possible that no other type of hui or Māori gathering can be as intimidating for non-Māori as a tangihanga, yet, paradoxically, the tangihanga is one of the main hui that friends and families should attend and work colleagues often have to attend to represent the company or organisation.

I think it is intimidating for a number of reasons but one main one undoubtably is that Māori and Pasifika peoples fundamentally see and treat the process and the philosophies surrounding death very differently from Pākehā. I'm not judging if one way is better than the other. I'm merely providing information and insights into Māori ways of dealing with death, and sometimes that may mean comparing it with the dominant culture in Aotearoa New Zealand, which is Pākehā.

While death is not quite so important as life in te ao Māori, it is incredibly important. It is tapu. It is honoured and respected and treated with reverence. To those of us that are immersed in our Māori world, the way Pākehā people, in general, deal with a deceased loved one seems, at best, fleeting, and at worst, disrespectful. But much like our disparate ways of dealing with the elderly, it is part of the fabric of our individual cultures. In te ao Māori, elders are venerated for their lived experience of te reo, tikanga and the world. This is knowledge, wisdom and truth that can't be merely read about; it has to be lived, and mana is gained from that. In the Pākehā world, it seems that the opposite is true. As a generalisation, it can appear to Māori that elders are sometimes cast out to fade away in retirement homes where they won't be seen and are the responsibility of others who are paid to care for them. While you will find a few elderly Māori folk in rest homes and retirement villages, they generally have no whānau to look after them or they need the specialised medical care that only these providers can give. If at all possible, it is generally preferred that whānau take care of kaumātua.

Inevitably, elders pass away and whānau and supporters have to prepare for the tangihanga.

The tangihanga process

You may have noticed the word 'tangi' as the root word. This literally means to cry, to lament, so the tangihanga, colloquially called a 'tangi', is the process of lamentation, of grieving. Some iwi refer to it as an 'uhunga', which also means to weep and lament. The burial itself is called the nehunga. Variations of the burial terms include 'te rā nehu', the 'tanumanga', the 'tāpuketanga' and others.

There is so much preparation to a tangihanga, especially a large one where hundreds and sometimes thousands of mourners are expected, that it deserves its own book so let's skip ahead to what is most likely involved for the non-Māori person.

SHARING GRIEF AND BEING SUPPORTED

Diametrically opposed to the 'keep it quiet', or 'it's a private time' viewpoint that many Pākehā people have,

Māori who are strong in their language and culture usually prefer to share the experience and find comfort and support in that sharing. This helps them through the stages of grieving until they come to accept what has happened and can move forward. This is why the tangihanga lasts three days. So that the 'kirimate', the bereaved family — literally the same DNA or skin (kiri) as the deceased (mate) — have time to shed tears and share their grief with each other and other mourners who arrive at the marae to pay their respects. This is the foundation of the Māori support system when there is a bereavement. It was eloquently summed up in a whakataukī from pre-colonisation times:

> **'Tukuna ngā roimata kia heke, whiua te hūpē,**
> **ka haruru te tapuwae ki te marae, ka ea, ka ea'**
> **'Let the tears flow, let the mucus run freely,**
> **gather together at the marae to share in**
> **support of one another and the dearly departed**
> **will be honoured.'**

There goes all the macho, 'once were warriors' rubbish out the window! Yes, the tūpuna were tough when they needed to be, but this traditional whakataukī is saying that when it is time to grieve, you must let it out, you must express your emotions and that there is peace in that. Note that there is no delineation hinted at between males and females in this whakataukī. Some of the most heartfelt sadness at a loss was expressed by men in their compositions of waiata tangi (traditional laments). It doesn't say 'men don't cry' or 'keep a stiff upper lip'; it says let out your emotions when it is appropriate to do so and share your grief and be supported.

This is how Māori, Pacific peoples and many indigenous societies have learnt to cope with loss over millennia. My experience is that this ethos of not repressing emotions but channelling them appropriately over a long period of time in the company and support of whānau and friends is not only healthy but essential for good mental health and well-being.

While the restrictions brought about by Covid-19 have been a great difficulty for all the world, it has been especially trying for the Māori grieving process. During lockdown there were many who passed away, so for a people whose very well-being is dependent on sharing in sorrow together, it hit especially hard. For a people that value being there in person, where face to face is the norm, it was incredibly difficult having to farewell beloved figures in te ao Māori via Zoom and social media platforms.

WHEN TO ATTEND

In order to follow a chain of events as an example, let's suppose a Māori colleague from work has passed away and your organisation feels a duty to go to the tangi or just wants representatives there to pay their respects. There are many aspects of tikanga to address, but I feel one of the most vital ones is that whoever is going to the tangihanga should not go on the last day only. It is fine to go on the last day, especially if there is a desire to go to the service, if the party from work has visited previously, but it is severely frowned upon to only go on the last day. Some Māori whānau are more forgiving than others and might say something like: 'It's okay. They don't know the tikanga.' But others who are less forgiving may remark: 'Kua tae mai ki te kai' — 'How typical, they have turned up just in time to eat.'

You are strongly encouraged to attend the tangi in the first two days as this is the time when speeches can be made and eloquent eulogies given. The last day is mainly for the funeral service, the actual burial and the eventual focus on the future for the whānau.

It is best to go during the day, but not just because this is during business hours. Some iwi avoid welcoming manuhiri at night, though this seems to be becoming less prominent these days as visitors and whānau increasingly have to travel from overseas.

BEING PREPARED

The second imperative is to be prepared. Again, the more forgiving whānau and marae members may just brush it off if the party from work is not prepared, but some may not. Much like the government minister in the previous chapter who had not prepared properly for a Māori event with a staunch Māori audience, it is best to prepare to go to a tangihanga.

ENGAGE AN EXPERT

Being prepared entails getting an appropriate kaikaranga and kaikōrero to handle, on your behalf, the various tikanga aspects. Unless your work has spent a good amount of time on the marae or they have been taught quite extensively what to do in Māori situations and at tangihanga, it is always best to have mātanga tikanga (tikanga experts) to bring you onto the marae. Many employers these days are contracting or even hiring full time people for these roles to help with their engagement with te ao Māori.

I have seen possibly hundreds of Pākehā and Tauiwi people come to the marae to pay tribute to the deceased, and the vast majority were much like fish out of water, not knowing what to do, in what order and when. This awkwardness is alleviated greatly if you have someone knowledgeable in Māori customs and protocols to guide your party.

I am not advocating that you should leave this knowledge only to these mātanga. Employees should get familiar with tangihanga protocols too so they can go to show their respect in person. The reality, however, is that the kaupapa is the deceased and the last thing that anyone wants is to embarrass themselves or distract from the gravitas of the situation and the focus on the tūpāpaku (deceased), so being prepared in what to do and when is strongly advised.

KOHA

Another part of preparation is to have a koha. This contribution to the whānau pani (another term for the bereaved family) and/or the marae is essential.

How much should one give? As individuals, most

Contributing what you can

As a person who has grown up poor, there were plenty of times when my contribution had to be physical labour or other contributions. I have sold clothes so that I would have a couple of dollars to be able to put into the koha envelope.

Once, when I was a teenager in the 1980s, I had a mere two dollars to last me to the end of the week. The marae whānau was going to a hui and a person was chosen to gather a contribution to the koha from everyone going. When the collector got to me, I put one dollar in the envelope. That was half of what I had for the rest of the week. But the collector announced out loud in front of everyone that 'It's at least two dollars from everyone!' I was so embarrassed that I put the other dollar I had into the koha. Little did I know that our kaumātua, a wonderful, generously spirited man, had seen this happen and observed my embarrassment. He gathered everyone together and lectured the collector on how people were free to contribute what they could, based on what they could afford. The collector visibly went red in his own embarrassment, possibly because he was quite rich and he had only put in two dollars.

The kaumātua and others of the marae whānau always looked after me following that incident, knowing that I had little to contribute financially, and they never put me in that position again. I resolved then and there that my koha to the whānau would be loyalty, energy and effort. If they needed someone to do the dishes, clean the toilets or play the guitar, I would be there. I would learn everything and hold the knowledge that they taught me so that I could one day share it with others. And sharing it with others is what I have done ever since.

people are not expected to contribute hundreds or thousands of dollars for a koha, but if a workplace or an organisation wants to show respect at a tangihanga, I believe it is only fitting to contribute a large koha. As an individual, think about how long you are staying, how many meals you are having, how much you want to show your respect, and err on the side of generosity. As a workplace, company or organisation, think of the same and err on the side of the very generous!

This is assuming that you have some money to gift. If you are not able to give any money, you may be able to give your time, energy or effort to help.

WHO SHOULD ATTEND?

Now, in the tangi example, let's say you are sorting out the logistics of getting your co-workers prepared to go. At this stage, the question is often: who should go? Can we afford to have workers missing a day of work? Maybe only the deceased's immediate team members should go? In the final analysis, the bosses have to make those decisions, of course, but I would suggest that this is the time to be thinking with the heart and not the head. Whoever genuinely wants to go in order to acknowledge the tūpāpaku and perhaps the contribution that they made to the company, their work lives, or even their personal lives, should go. It is not a day of missing work. This is work. And should be in work time. This is connecting with te ao Māori. The local tangata whenua will remember the company coming to show respect and this is the basis with which to forge relationships.

CARDS AND FLOWERS

Feel free to get a card and sign it from everyone and/or take flowers. The main thing for the whānau will be that you turned up in person as a sign of respect, but this is also a nice gesture. These can be given to the whānau pani or are often laid at the feet of the casket.

ON THE MARAE

So, the bosses have agreed that this is indeed part of building networks with the local iwi/hapū/marae, it is in work time and as many workers as possible can go and the koha reflects that. (Keep in mind that we are just going through a fairly typical tangihanga scenario without the added complications of Covid-19 restrictions, quarantining or attending via Zoom.)

You have found the marae (some marae are quite out of the way) and you are ready to go on. As mentioned, it is best if you have your own kaikōrero and kaikaranga, but sometimes, especially if it is a sudden death, this may not be possible in time. In that case, you can wait until other people arrive, join their group and go on with them. If this is the case, I would recommend you introduce yourselves, hongi and shake hands and if the hosts have a speaker, give the koha to him to lay down during his whaikōrero. This can feel difficult, parting with the money and trusting that it will go to the right place, but unless you have your own kaikōrero, usually the last speaker will lay down the koha so the options are fairly limited.

Note that more and more marae are becoming open to giving receipts for koha, especially when it is from a business, but it is still mostly considered bad form to ask for one at a tangi. Again, if you have a relationship with the local hapū, this is not such an awkward conversation, but be prepared to write it off as 'networking'. Because it is, and having earned the respect of the local tangata whenua by turning up in person and giving a generous koha, you want to maintain that mana-enhancing relationship.

MOVING ONTO THE MARAE

Much like the process of the pōwhiri previously discussed, the same actions happen in the same order. The local people deliver the karanga, the visitors respond and you begin to walk on slowly to the marae. The only difference in this process is probably something that you can't understand unless you speak te reo. The karanga will have an added focus on the kaupapa, the purpose of the hui, which is, of course, the tūpāpaku.

The word 'tūpāpaku' has different iwi interpretations in its etymology, but in Taranaki, reflecting the tikanga of maintaining humility, it means to stand (tū) shallowly (pāpaku), i.e. humbly. The notion is that the deceased lying in state can hear all the complimentary statements made about them in the whaikōrero, but they will never stand to acknowledge them and be thought of as whakahīhī — conceited. Quite a beautiful interpretation of a natural state of being, I think, but a typical Taranaki one.

As the group walks onto the marae, you might stop for a short while to remember tūpuna that have gone before, and then, gradually, everyone takes a seat, men in front ready to begin the whaikōrero.

There could be variations depending on where you are, whether the protocols are conducted inside the wharenui or sometimes a specific tent, or whether it is raining and cold which might be harmful to the kaumātua. Commonly, though, this is the order of things.

Seeing a deceased person, in an open casket, can be harrowing for people who aren't used to it. To those within te ao Māori, it is quite normal. An undertaker once asked me if I was okay to see the dead body of the whanaunga (relative) I had come to see. I told her that I had probably seen more dead bodies than she had.

WHAIKŌRERO AND WAIATA

The speechmaking and singing begin in the patterns that I have discussed in Chapter 3. The poetry expressed in both the karanga and the whaikōrero performed by the skilled practitioner is breathtaking and, at a tangi, will be focused on the deceased and their whānau. It can also contain whakapapa, mihi, history, wondrous wise whakataukī, brilliantly executed haka and ngeri (haka chants performed without uniform actions) and a slew of metaphoric comparisons that would make Shakespeare kākāriki with envy (see Chapter 4 for insights into the art of Māori oratory).

Generally, if the tūpāpaku is lying on the mahau (veranda) of the wharenui, the whaikōrero and protocols will be performed outside, but quite often the mate (deceased) will be inside the wharenui, lying at the base of the back wall (again, the placement of the tūpāpaku is done according to iwi tradition so it can vary).

One thing I should mention here is that some whānau, for various reasons, may take their dear departed to a house instead of the marae where the same tikanga will be enacted. If that is the case, just follow the same procedures.

Just as in the normal pōwhiri, the final speaker will lay down the koha concluding the speeches (see Chapter 2 for variations on tikanga depending on the rohe).

VARIATIONS

The weight of the tangi and the strict or loose adherence to tikanga is largely dependent on the region in which it is being held, the people running the paepae and protocols, and whether the tangi is at a marae or not. Commonly, the tangi is seen as one of the last bastions of authentic tikanga Māori so this is why it is best to have kaumātua or kaikōrero worked out beforehand to navigate these sometimes choppy waters and to lead people on in relative cultural safety, especially if the manuhiri are newcomers to the marae.

If the tangihanga is being held at someone's house the protocols can be a bit looser, but it depends on what the whānau wants and what their supporters want. At one tangi, the deceased was a very staunch kaumātua who didn't want any English spoken during the procedures. This was vehemently enforced by the supporters of the whānau who wanted to honour the last wishes of the departed kaumātua. The tangi was taking place inside the wharenui so when some manuhiri turned up to pay tribute and they were told that only te reo was to be spoken inside the whare, their speaker stood up, walked outside and delivered his eulogy in English from there. In that way, the tikanga was fulfilled and the manuhiri could say what they wanted to in the language that they were more familiar with.

Of course, these are the subtleties of tikanga that can only be traversed by the holders and wielders of this knowledge. The uninitiated wouldn't normally have to deal with anything quite so unique.

CONCLUSION — HONGI

As per the normal pōwhiri, the formal kawa ceremony concludes with the hongi (keep in mind the variations that can occur in different areas) and the hongi line should steer you towards the bereaved family and, eventually, your co-worker who is lying in state there. Hopefully you are led by a kaumātua but if not, it is nice if the work leadership can front foot this process. Going around the kirimate, they will hongi, kiss or hug you — which of these occurs largely depends on your relationship with them and the deceased worker in the past. Whatever transpires, they will definitely appreciate the gesture in you turning up in person.

Obviously, common sense should take precedence so if the worker died at work because of negligence and the grieving widow and family blame you or your co-workers, it might not be appropriate to go!

But let's assume that this is not the case and you have turned up as a sign of respect for the many long hours worked by the person and because you want to embody the goodwill emblazoned in your mission statement.

APPROACHING THE TŪPĀPAKU

Whether the casket is open or not and whether it is on the mahau or inside the wharenui, most frequently the immediate family will surround the tūpāpaku. Often if there is a widow, male or female, they will be situated right next to the body. As you hongi/kiss/hug the family you approach the body of the deceased worker. What to do now? Many people just look and silently acknowledge the person and it is nice to think of a fond memory while doing this. For many Māori it is important to hongi the deceased person, but this is one of those tikanga that many whānau easily forgive Pākehā people for not doing in recognition that it is simply not usually a done thing in Pākehā culture. I have performed the hongi with many tūpāpaku, especially those I felt particularly close to, because it is the last time you will have the opportunity to do so.

You would now usually move to the other side of the casket and continue to hongi/kiss/hug with the rest of the family until there is no one left to hongi. Occasionally, there is a pause here when you may be able to just sit down and talk to the family less formally, but often you will be ushered out into the wharekai to partake in a shared kai while more manuhiri arrive. There is often a bucket or source of water in between these two houses which people use to dip their hands in and sprinkle themselves with water. This is a tikanga about removing the tapu of the tūpāpaku before going into the noa world of the wharekai.

And this mainly concludes the trip to the tangi.

AFTER THE EVENT

With the protocols fulfilled and the company well represented, you have done what you set out to do which is to show your respect for the tūpāpaku and show your support for the family at this tough time. So, it may be straight back to the office. But can I encourage you to take some time out as a work whānau. Go and have a coffee together and talk about what just happened and how you felt. It is an important experience that you just shared. Don't underplay its significance. It can bring you closer as a team better than any retreat or course on leadership can do, while handled badly, without a bit of time to digest, it can leave negative feelings, especially if you have gone to all the trouble of doing this wonderful thing and the next thing the higher-ups are cracking the whip with 'get back to work!' If your workplace is interested in leadership and not just management, you will take some time to give mana to the experience.

An enriching experience

This discussion is a simple explanation of the frequent order of procedures and actions. There are so many associated tikanga and rituals before, during and after the tangihanga that it could be a PhD thesis in itself (and probably has been), but here are some further whakamārama (explanations).

There is a groundswell movement at the moment encouraging the use of more traditional and natural materials used in tangihanga and a move away from funeral homes. This includes natural alternatives to preserving the deceased's body, naturally made platforms for the body to lie on that can be carried easily to the urupā for burial and a woven flax 'casket' called a kahu whakatere that envelops the tūpāpaku. While not yet commonplace in most areas, this kaupapa is gaining momentum in te ao Māori.

You may see a lot of greenery worn by people and hoisted onto the wharenui during tangi. The most common plant leaf used is kawakawa (a native pepper tree), but different plant leaves are used in different areas. This tikanga is complex, but in very simple terms the leaves represent both life and death: one side representing each but part of the same leaf. For many Māori, we carry our dearly departed and ancestors wherever we go. They are part of us.

As much as possible, I have gone through the most common order of tikanga associated with a tangi, but this is a very basic template and different iwi, hapū, marae, rohe and even whānau sometimes have very different tikanga depending on who has the experience and the mana to determine it.

You may think that I over emphasise the non-homogeneous aspect of Māoritanga, but it has been my vast experience that many non-Māori, especially Pākehā, have a difficult time when they have expected one thing and another thing happens. And then another, and another until there is no plan left and you just have to cope and go with the flow. Not all Pākehā people, but many. One Māori person said to me, 'Pākehā people can't be spontaneous. It's not in their nature.' While that is the broadest of generalisations, the truth that it hints at is that Māori things, kaupapa Māori and te ao Māori very much involve being agile, pivoting when the unplanned happens. Possibly because we have had to be since colonisation. And in direct proportion, Pākehā people, things and kaupapa have basically been in charge and running the country since the 1840s so stepping out of the Pākehā comfort zone of knowing what is happening all the time, of having decision-making power, of speaking the only language you know is incredibly intimidating. So, once again, I commend you for reading this book, wanting to learn more and especially if you have been to a marae or a tangihanga. Ka pai. Good on you.

One Pākehā person remarked to me that going to the marae for a tangi was like going to China where he didn't know what was happening, what to do and what to say. But he also said that he left that experience culturally richer and feeling like he had a better appreciation of te ao Māori and couldn't wait to learn more.

I hope that is the case with the readers of this book.

Chapter 7

Tikanga — doing things differently

PROBABLY ONE OF THE MOST asked questions I've had in my life and career is basically, 'How do I not cause offence to Māori people?' The question comes from a good place and a good heart and a well-intentioned curiosity.

It is tricky to answer though. We are talking about different cultural norms, differing ways of thinking and being. How we see the world and interact with it is different. Some things are similar, but so much is distinct that there is no one all-encompassing answer apart from learning about each other and trying to be respectful. However, in this chapter I'll provide a little help — he paku āwhina — with some do's and don'ts.

Tapu and noa

I've picked up a few shortcuts over the years that may help at least mitigate the circumstances that can lead to causing offence. Most of these examples are based on different worldviews and concepts like mana, tapu and noa.

In te reo and tikanga classes of Pākehā and Tauiwi that I have taught, when I ask the question 'Who washes their tea towels with their clothes?' there are usually at least a couple of brave souls who put their hands up. Quite often most people slink back into the comfort of the group, knowing that they most likely won't be chosen individually to answer and therefore run the risk of embarrassment at giving the 'wrong' answer.

The truth is that there is no wrong answer; it's just that our distinctive cultures have different mindsets and worldviews, and you have to embrace and respect that.

For Māori people who live in te ao Māori, you never wash your tea towels with your clothes.

Before I explain why, have a pause here in reading and try to come up with an answer to this yourself, given some of the examples and stories I have gone through in previous chapters.

If you guessed that the practice of not washing tea towels together with clothes, bedding or even shower towels in te ao Māori is based on the beliefs of tapu and noa, you would be right. Even some Māori who practise this tikanga aren't aware why they do it. If you ask them, they will often say 'because it just doesn't feel right' or 'it's yucky' or 'unhygienic' and especially 'because my mum told me not to'.

THE BODY

The real reason why this might 'feel yucky' is because of the principles of tapu and noa. The body is tapu and the head is the most tapu part. Anything that comes into contact with the body and especially the head is generally considered tapu. Clothes, bedding and shower towels all come into close contact with the body so become tapu.

The tea towels are associated with kai, which is noa, free from tapu, so the two should not mix. In simple terms, having the two concepts clash would be disrespecting tapu so it is not generally done. What this means in practical terms is that tea towels are most often washed separately and quite often in a separate bucket or dedicated washing machine. Think about how difficult this is when a Māori person is in accommodation here or overseas that only has a kitchen sink and no access to a washing machine!

Associated with the above example is this one: keep cleaning materials for the bathroom and kitchen separate. So, for instance, don't use the same mop that cleans the kitchen floor to clean the bathroom or toilet floor. Don't use the same cloth to clean the kitchen sink as the cloth that cleans the bathroom sink and so on.

STEPPING OVER PEOPLE

Another tikanga that comes from the concept of tapu and noa and has earned a quick admonishment many a time when it is done wrong is this: try not to step over anybody. Now, that sounds like a pretty easy job. How often do you ever have to walk over or step over someone else? Perhaps this doesn't come up at work a lot, but it does occur in a person's house or certainly on the marae. People may be lying on a mattress or have their legs extended and it is easy to forget. But like not sitting on a table (see below), this comes from the concept that the body is tapu so it is a definite no-no to step over anybody else's. This extends to bedding: try not to step on or over this, especially pillows. Anything that is associated with the head is especially tapu. The head is considered so tapu for some people that they collect their hair at the barber or hairdressers and take it home and bury it.

This isn't just some archaic protocol from yesteryear that should be done away with. The idea that the body is tapu and that the head is the most tapu part is ancient in the Māori world, but it is also practical. If two toa (warriors) met and fought, they would protect their heads.

The ūpoko (head) is the centre of reason, the place of memories, and holds the capacity for learning, to retain and recall whakapapa.

This is why servers in restaurants and at the marae should never pass food over someone's head. Again, food which is noa, without tapu, and things that are tapu, sacred, should not mix, in Māori thinking. This is why hats or combs and hairbrushes should not be left on a table or even lying about the place.

The ultimate swear word in te reo Māori (yes, there are swear words in te reo; we will be exploring them more in the next chapter) is 'pokokōhua'. This can mean 'to curse' but literally means to boil a person's head. This is hard to grasp as anything other than a silly nonsense in the non-Māori world, but it is the worst insult in the Māori one. The implication is that the person who is being insulted is going to have the most tapu part of their body boiled and made noa and harkens back to pre-colonisation times when to be eaten in an act of cannibalism and one's bones used for tools was the epitome of offence and could often lead to acts of vengeance for generations. It is because of this sensitivity that it is a good idea to not mix the head and food together, even in metaphors. There are a few examples of this in English, but probably the clearest one to illustrate the point is the phrase: 'I just want to pick your brains . . .' Never say that to a Māori person!

Easy enough to do, isn't it? Don't kick yourself too hard if you have said this to someone Māori before. You can't possibly be expected to know things like this because there simply isn't any way of knowing these concepts and tikanga unless you have had the opportunity to learn from someone in the know or you have read it before in educational materials on tikanga Māori.

RESPECTING TŪPĀPAKU

Have you ever seen a hearse with a tūpāpaku (deceased person) in it go past, and Māori people extinguishing their cigarettes? Obviously, smoking is not healthy so, yes, people shouldn't be doing it in the first place, but if Māori people are smoking, you can still observe this tikanga, even now. I have seen this many times (not so much in recent years as smoking goes out of fashion) and I have asked many times why they felt they needed to put their cigarettes out before the hearse came past. Like the tea towel and clothes mixing example, most often people don't know why; they are just compelled to do it by an event in a distant memory, it feels like 'the right thing to do' or 'because my mother/father/uncle/ aunt/kaumātua said so'. As I have spent a lot of my career explaining the reasoning behind tikanga, I have found it ever fascinating that although they may not know why or they can't articulate why, a lot of Māori still observe these tikanga in a practical way. Again, the reason is that there is a conflict between tapu and noa. The hearse and the tūpāpaku are tapu.

While cigarettes clearly don't offer any nutritional value, they are considered 'kai'. Perhaps because of the nature of chewing tobacco in the past or just because they go in the mouth and the smoke goes into the body, any sort of smoking, vaping, a pipe or the like is thought of as kai and therefore is noa. Like fire and water, tapu and noa don't tend to mix well.

TABLES

Time for a classic. This is such a common one, especially at work. Don't sit or lean your behind on a table. Many a Māori person has had the slightly embarrassing job (or slightly empowering job depending on the person) of somehow letting the person sitting or leaning know that this is not appropriate. Again, based on the concept of tapu and noa, the body part is tapu and the table is where the kai goes so is therefore noa. Mahi (work) is noa so this applies to work desks too. Interestingly, this is another tikanga Māori that is being adopted by non-Māori as part of the shaping of a modern Aotearoa New Zealand identity, especially in the workplace.

Show some sensitivity

Try not to assume all Māori people are connected to their language and culture. As mentioned in Chapter 1, the vast majority of Māori are still not brought up speaking their language at home, living immersed in their tikanga and ideologies. And this can be a sensitive subject or source of embarrassment.

If you learn some te reo or tikanga, take care in how you embrace that with disconnected Māori folk. Many Māori people who are immersed in te ao Māori appreciate a respectful, humble effort to say a well-pronounced word or phrase, but to the disenfranchised Māori person

Tikanga and empowerment

I should explain why informing someone that sitting on a table is inappropriate can be empowering. Some Pākehā especially have had the experience of being 'told off'. The usually (but not exclusively) Māori informant may not have been terribly gentle or may even have been abrasive in telling the person that their behaviour is wrong according to tikanga Māori.

Of course, the experience is subjective depending on the urgency and vehemence of the 'teller' and the resilience and open-mindedness of the recipient, but what I have noticed is that if you don't feel heard or very powerful, it can feel good to momentarily have the power to inform someone else about an aspect of your culture of which they are unaware.

I have also observed that people who are used to understanding how the world works, having decision-making power and being in control can overreact when they feel out of their comfort zone, uninformed, disadvantaged or not in control. This can be a common reaction when Pākehā go to a marae. Not so much Tauiwi. People from overseas often feel that it is an interesting part of Aotearoa New Zealand culture to visit a marae and they don't feel the same level of inadequacy when visiting as they haven't been brought up in this country. Pākehā people, however, at least the many who I have taught or brought to the marae, seem to find this very intimidating, especially if they are required to stay the night.

In feedback from Pākehā upon return from the marae, most often they are elated, feel closer to tangata whenua and an Aotearoa New Zealand identity. They are glad they did it and are much more likely to go again and feel more comfortable in doing so, but almost universally they were reluctant to go, intimidated by perhaps not knowing everything that was happening, especially if there is a lot of te reo spoken. They felt disadvantaged and not in control.

While I understand this, I struggle to feel too much sympathy because of one major difference in our situations. Choice. Ninety-nine per cent of the time, Pākehā people have a choice. I have seen Pākehā leave the marae or even just a Māori situation if they don't feel comfortable. Sometimes they just won't come in the first place and that's their choice. There isn't usually a consequence to this. In work situations, the boss might encourage staff to attend a Māori function, but it is very rare that people are reprimanded for not going. Even if they do go begrudgingly, as soon as it is over, be it two hours or two days, they happily go back to their lives usually content in the knowledge that they won't have to do that again or if they do it was for a short time and they survived so if needs be, they could do it again.

Māori don't have this choice. We can't 'opt out' of living and working in a generally 'mainstream' environment. Yes, there are a few areas in the country with high Māori populations and some kaupapa-based workplaces around, but even those are surrounded by the dominant culture, and it is not Māori culture. I have been on the marae for weeks on end, speaking only in te reo, but as soon as you leave you are confronted with the stark reality that you need petrol for the car so, naturally, you have to revert to English. You are no longer in the environment in which you feel the most comfortable.

Wearing your Tino Rangatiratanga (Māori

independence and autonomy) shirt garners stares and sometimes outright hostility, and you are constantly reminded that you are not in control, you are not able to ask for parāoa (bread) and speak and live in the way of your ancestors. Sometimes, e hoa mā, that just sucks.

this can be quite 'triggering' in feelings of inadequacy. There can be an innate belief in some that they should somehow understand te ao Māori intuitively because they are Māori, even if they weren't brought up within this enchanting but sometimes beguiling, nuanced world. People can know on an intellectual level that this isn't logical, but it is still a prominent misconception even on a subconscious level. And people can react in a negative way instead of admitting that they don't know.

So, much like looking forward in the hongi line to see what is happening ahead in order to predict whether it will be one press of the nose or two, move slowly in this realm, testing out a small word or phrase and gauging reaction. Don't call attention to yourself with it, just treat it like it is an everyday thing for you that you do to show your respect for things Māori. Like pronouncing 'kia ora' well or saying a Māori name or word properly.

DON'T OVERDO IT

I have met so many Pākehā and Tauiwi with the best intentions that tend to know a little bit of tikanga or te reo and undermine their well-meant intent by overdoing it or relying on that one thing they know.

An example might be when Māori people interact with that Pākehā person who insists on always performing the hongi each time they meet. Even Māori don't necessarily hongi each other every time they meet! Especially if they know each other well or they saw each other not that long ago. Here is the good intention that overdone becomes an annoyance. The answer is simple: let the Māori person determine the type of greeting. Just approach, making it clear that you are wanting to 'say hello' and the Māori person will determine how that should go. If they haven't seen you for a while or it is a more formal situation, they may choose to hongi you. Or it might be an awhi (hug) or a handshake, or, in these times of global pandemics, it might be a wave or a greeting from a safe distance. The point is to let the Māori person 'call the shots' when it comes to greeting. You will find that a rhythm is soon established and it is no longer unclear how the situation will go.

Language and pronunciation

Probably, by now, this will come as a surprise to no one but a really important 'do' is: do get pronunciation right. By mastering the long and short vowels, the consonant blends of 'wh' and 'ng' and the ever-tricky rolled 'r' sound, this is the number one short cut to a respectful relationship with the Māori language, Māori people and te ao Māori in general. Combine this with the casual humility of routine for your everyday speech patterns and you are bound to enhance your relationship with the tangata whenua of Aotearoa.

In one of my various professional development opportunities, the tutor kept calling me 'Kurī'. My name is Keri. Pretty close, right? Every time he asked me a question, or wanted a comment from me, he would preface it with 'Kurī, tell me about ...' I could never really answer him concisely because I was so distracted by his mispronunciation. After the third time I took him aside and corrected his pronunciation and told him why I had not been able to answer him to the best of my ability — the word 'kurī' means 'dog'! He was embarrassed but as he was a good man and a good tutor, he quickly corrected himself and never made the mistake again. By having good pronunciation, the potential for insult or embarrassment declines exponentially and you can instead concentrate on enjoying relationships.

Now, you may be thinking, 'Why didn't you just correct him the first time?' This is another reality for Māori people with Māori names. Most of the time you have to decide if it is 'worth it' to correct the mistake. In this case I waited until the third time because it was a new relationship, I had never met the tutor before and a potential conflict or sour start to the relationship was not desirable. He was in the dominant position as the professional development class tutor so the potential for him to be embarrassed and lose some respect from the class members with whom he was attempting to establish a rapport was on my mind. I also didn't want to possibly jeopardise my generally positive relationship with the other class members by bringing something that could be perceived as negative into the class at this early stage. And I hoped that he might not use my name or he might hear someone else say my name properly and self-correct.

To be honest, if the accidental mispronunciation of my name hadn't meant anything, if it was a nonsensical jumble of sounds not causing offence in its absurdity, I might not have bothered to say anything and just put up with it for the day, expecting to never see the tutor again and chalking it up to just one of the many hundreds of times someone has got my name wrong.

This is a process faced by every Māori person, every day when they encounter a person that doesn't pronounce Māori words and, therefore, Māori names correctly. We have to inevitably ask ourselves 'Is it worth it?' Sometimes it is, but other times, it really isn't. I recently bumped into a Māori woman who I used to go to school with. I have not seen her for almost forty years. I remember her name was mispronounced at school so when we saw each other we caught up for a minute. She reintroduced herself: 'Hey, remember me, we used to go to school together. I'm . . .' — and she used her misshapen 'Māori' name. It had not changed in nearly forty years. In that entire time she had just resigned herself to putting up with it so much so that, in essence, that was now her name. For her, telling everyone she had met over the years her real name had not been worth it. My serendipitous meeting with her after all these years, while enjoyable, was laced with bittersweetness.

SUPPORTING POSITIVE CHANGE

This is where good pronunciation deals with all of that history. It is one of the things that Pākehā, Tauiwi and Māori who are disconnected from their worldviews can do to support where this country is heading. It feels like the country is moving away from the time when it was just easier to fit in by mispronouncing your ancestral name and towards a more enlightened time when everyone is more informed about te ao Māori and the nation is much better for it.

Imagine if my school friend had had the respectfully curious, like yourself reading this book, to pronounce her name properly at every turn, and perhaps encourage others to pronounce it properly as well. I know from experience that this is extremely empowering and something that everyone can choose to do. Kia toa! (Be brave, be courageous).

PLURALS

Try not to add the letter 's' to Māori words, e.g. iwis, hapūs, maraes. Many words in te reo Māori are both singular and plural. It is dependent on the definitive before the word to determine whether it is in the plural or not, e.g. te marae (the marae), ngā marae (the many marae). Seemingly, this is a small grammatical correction but they do add up. Good pronunciation, not using 's' for Māori words, an open mind, being respectfully curious, these are foundational building blocks to create relationships with te ao Māori me ōna tāngata — the Māori world and its citizens.

GREETING ELDERS
GREETING ELDERS

Do greet kaumātua (male or female elder) with the phrase 'Tēnā koe' (greetings to the person I am speaking to). This is slightly more formal than 'Kia ora' and is a show of respect. Greet two kaumātua with 'Tēnā kōrua' and use 'Tēnā koutou' for three or more people.

Continue to learn

Do learn from any errors you may make. It is near to impossible to explore a culture and language unfamiliar to you without making a faux pas here and there. These are usually understandable and forgivable. What is more hōhā (tiresome) is if a person doesn't learn from them and makes the same mistake over and over.

The old people had many whakataukī on the subject, such as: 'Ko te weka i maunu i te māhanga, e kore a muri e hokia' — 'If the weka escapes the snare, it will not return to it'.

I once was told to go and pick up a koha laid down by the manuhiri (this is often a sign that a young person is being taught the art of whaikōrero and is part of the apprenticeship). It was a windy day and the speaker from the manuhiri had put the koha on the ground and placed a rock on top of it to weigh it down. I tossed the rock aside and retrieved the koha and then walked backwards to the speakers' bench as is the tikanga so that you don't turn your back on the manuhiri.

After the hui was over and the manuhiri had left, the kaumātua gathered us together for a debrief. Every opportunity was taken to learn something new. I wasn't told off, but I was told, quite clearly, in front of all participants, that if a koha is laid down with a rock on top of it, the rock is part of the koha and you should bring that back to the paepae as well as the envelope with the money in it. Who would've thought? I was very embarrassed, but it was part of the learning process.

A lot of learning under tikanga Māori is experiential learning. There is theory, but emphasis is placed on the practical. You have to be able to 'do' in te ao Māori, not just talk about it. I think that it is part of the test of mettle when you are being taught. It can be tough, but the old people know that if you don't build up your resilience, you will find it very difficult coping with the challenges that naturally come with leading. 'Ka whati te tī, ka wana te tī, ka rito te tī' — 'When the cabbage tree breaks in two, it eventually builds itself up and grows again.' This whakataukī encourages us to have resilience like the cabbage tree.

There is a whakataukī for every occasion or situation. Do find some online or in the many whakataukī books that are available. There is real wisdom in these spoken treasures.

Do practise a pepeha, which were discussed in Chapter 5.

Tangihanga

Do go to tangihanga. Obviously, I'm not advocating to just randomly go to any tangi, but if you have an association with the deceased or their whānau and you want to show your support, go along. It would pay to be prepared and have talked with people in the know to see if you need your own person to whaikōrero or karanga, but don't let these things put you off going. It is a sign of respect and aroha to turn up in person. (See the previous chapter for more on tangihanga.)

In the home

In addition to not sitting or leaning on tables, and should the situation arise, not stepping over someone, there are other situations in the home governed by different tikanga.

BIRDS

Here is a tikanga that you may not be aware of. If a bird flies into your house, try to shoo it outside or catch it and let it out — easier said than done, but note that different birds represent different things to different iwi. The most common tikanga like this is that if a fantail enters into your house, it is best to try to catch it and let it outside. For many iwi the fantail represents an omen of misfortune or death so it is treated with respect, especially if it gets indoors.

This tikanga is derived from a pūrākau (narrative legend) which states that the fantail is the bird that inadvertently caused the death of Māui, the ancestor hero who featured prominently in many pūrākau from tūpuna throughout the Pacific. Many iwi, hapū and whānau are associated with a particular bird so it is better to just try to send them all on their way.

SHOES

Do ask if you should take your shoes off when entering a home that belongs to a Māori person. Obviously, if there is a big pile of shoes at the front door, that is a fairly sure sign to leave your shoes there, but asking makes it clear. Some people are ever staunch about this but others, not so much.

ABIDE BY THE HOST'S CUSTOMS

And that brings up another point. Kia tae atu te tangata ki Roma, me mahi e ia tā te Roma i tono ai — when in Rome, do as the Romans do. Some people treat their home like a marae, complete with mattresses for guests, kai always at the ready and a pōwhiri when people visit, so try to go with the flow. It is relatively uncommon, but some people will put on a full pōwhiri at their house for every visitor while others may only do that for guests with great mana in te ao Māori. Some see it as their home and not the marae and don't have any welcoming processes there except for offering a cup of tea. Try to be prepared for any eventuality.

Contribute positively

This is just scratching the surface of tikanga, really. Different ways of doing things and seeing the world evolve naturally from any culture. And from any culture regional variations will occur. Māori tikanga reflects a fascinating worldview, filled with the intricacies of a multi-layered, thoughtful society that has had some hard lessons in survival from the past and is evolving into a positive future.

You, dear reader, are helping by reading this book. *Do* become more informed. Part of the intimidation of hui, tangihanga or the marae is the unknown. Read, go online, do courses, learn what you can from the sources that are accessible to you. And, if the opportunity arises, *do* go to the marae. Learn who the local iwi and hapū are and, if possible, what some of the local tikanga are (remember the example from Whanganui in Chapter 3).

Marae and Māori organisations are often looking for helpful support. If you have influence at work or decision-making power, why not advocate to sponsor the local waka ama (outrigger canoe) club or give a donation towards the local kapa haka (Māori culture club). This sort of support is always appreciated and often leads to better relationships with the tangata whenua.

Do celebrate that Aotearoa is changing for the better. Something that is encouraging is the fact that younger generations are growing up more informed, with much more of a relationship with te ao Māori. There is much less of a need to inform them of Māori do's and don'ts as they are growing up with that as part of everyday life. Of course, that doesn't go for all taiohi, but it certainly is more prominent these days and appears to be increasingly so. I was recently at Parihaka at a commemoration of the beginning of the Land Wars and many schools and youth groups were there with this as part of their learning and school curriculum. It was very rewarding seeing them listening to the discussions and also doing some dishes and supporting where they could. These are the generations that will lead in the space of a more equitable Aotearoa.

Kōkiri! Onward and upward!

Chapter 8
Tōna tūturutanga — restoring te ao Māori

Supposed sexism in te ao Māori

Whether it is ordinary, everyday people making comments on social media or well-known people like politicians commenting on TV and radio, there is an overabundance of people, who are generally not Māori, judging and then commenting on many aspects of te ao Māori. One aspect that seems to come up often is the perception that the Māori world is androcentric, that it is sexist, even misogynistic to a certain degree. This is rarely explored in any depth, though, or discussed in the public arena by people who know tikanga Māori, who are steeped in it, so I want to discuss a simple question in this chapter, 'Is te ao Māori sexist?' as part of providing more understanding of tikanga.

I imagine anyone interested in this book is most likely an intelligent person who is fascinated by the world and its myriad cultures, so while you probably don't need a definition of sexism, let's narrow it down a little so that we can test te ao Māori next to some basic criteria. Let's say that sexism is prejudice, stereotyping or discrimination based on gender. And, typically, this is against the female gender. In older language, this might be considered 'chauvinism'. In more modern language, this is sometimes referred to as 'toxic masculinity'. But, really, in the broad sense and for the sake of this book, sexism involves anything that boils down to a simple equation: male = positive, female = negative.

So, how do we answer this question?

As with many instances of tikanga in this book, I'll

start with the language. Is te reo Māori sexist? This book is written in English and you, the reader, must have a certain level of fluency in English so we will examine some aspects of both languages to provide a comparison.

TE KANGAKANGA — SWEARING

Have you ever thought about how much swearing in a language reveals about the worldviews intrinsic to the speakers of that language? Probably not. It's not the sort of thing one ponders on a daily basis. But it is quite revealing. In English, for example, in general the worldviews that are expressed boil down to four main themes: religion, anatomy, disgust and sexuality (sexuality in the wider sense, not partner attraction). I won't belabour the point, but most swear words and concepts would fit into these categories in English. Some clear examples are: 'damn' (blasphemous), 'dick' (anatomy), 'shit' (disgust) and 'wanker' (sexuality). If we narrow focus further on, say, anatomy, i.e. body parts/genitalia, inevitably we will find that the same old equation applies, male = positive while female = negative. The obvious example here is 'dick' versus 'pussy'. While 'being a dick' is not seen as positive, there is no apparent judgement on the power dynamic. If someone is 'being a pussy' they are considered weak, a wimp, the implication is that being compared to female genitalia is a serious insult to 'manliness' for men but also, strangely, this 'insult' is sometimes used for women too, the judgement being that they are behaving in a feeble, wimpy way.

Swearing in te reo Māori uses none of these concepts.

Kangakanga is based on a Māori way of seeing the world that was in Aotearoa before the introduction of the Bible and the inherent philosophies of the missionaries, religion and Pākehā people that arrived here, namely, a concept that we have encountered before, tapu and noa. Swear words or words of insult are based on a premise of removing the tapu from the body (often the head, the most tapu part of the body) and consuming it, further adding insult to injury. The most common swear word in te reo Māori and a very heavy insult if aimed at someone is the word 'pokokōhua'. As mentioned earlier, this literally means to 'boil the head' (ūpoko — head, kōhua — boil/pot). In the Māori world, where the fabric of society runs on mana and tapu, many a battle has ensued over an insult like this. A whakataukī states 'He tao rākau, e taea te karo, he tao kī, e kore e taea' — 'A weapon's thrust can be parried, a barbed thrust of words cannot.'

This notion of tapu and noa is not just present in an age past. I once heard a kuia yell out 'pokokōhua!' when she hit her thumb using a hammer. She was actually a relatively gentle soul with a wonderful grasp of English, but when someone is under duress, they tend to revert to their first language. This was her equivalent to 'dammit!' or 'shit!'

Just contemplate, for a moment, the impact of what I have explained here. Swearing in te reo Māori is based on the indigenous worldview of tapu and noa. Think of all the swear words and curse words that are in general use in English throughout the world. There are so many that are based on a sexist or androcentric worldview. Even the phrase 'Son of a bitch' is somehow insulting a man by calling his mother a bitch! The closest insult to this in te reo might be a variation of 'koretake' or 'takekore', whereby the insult is that you don't know your whakapapa, but it isn't a judgement made based in sexism, i.e. 'You only know your mother's side of your whakapapa, how useless!' It is an insult based in a worldview where knowing your lineage is expected and something to be proud of.

Unfortunately, as I have explained in this book, te reo Māori is not in a strong, invulnerable position in this country. It is influenced by English greatly and if we can see above that English has an inherent sexism in it, that influence has penetrated into te reo. I have visited many kura kaupapa where te reo Māori is the dominant language of both instruction and the playground. I have been asked questions here like 'He aha te kupu Māori mō te bitch?' — 'What is the Māori word for bitch?' (I answered, 'There is none') and I have heard and observed boys listening to (mainly) American music full of insults to women and misogynistic worldviews and then talk among themselves repeating the same worldviews but in te reo Māori! These are the speakers and carriers of the Māori language for generations to come.

Whenever and wherever I can, I encourage tamariki and adults who are learning or speaking te reo to return to our traditional Māori worldviews, especially when it comes to the issue of sexism or androcentricity. Our narratives tell of Ranginui the sky father and Papatūānuku the earth mother. Here, there is balance.

If it was just Ranginui, the world would be out of equilibrium and simply wouldn't work.

Even when analysing some graphic descriptor swear words in te reo which may seem to use the 'disgust' aspect of English swearing, they are still harking back to tapu and noa:

kai a te kurī (dog food)
kai hamuti (to eat excrement)

This is how the lowest of the low is described. Not only is it kai (noa) but it is even less than that. It is merely food for a dog or, even lower than that, food which has already been processed through the body and come out the other end. It is harder to get more 'noa' than that. So even though these concepts might be disgusting, it is still based in a worldview of tapu and noa.

Note, Māori swearing is much more dependent on context and vehemence of delivery than the actual words. For example:

'Kei te aha tērā kai hamuti?' — 'What is that silly bugger up to?'
'Kāti te tiro makutu mai, kai hamuti!' — 'Stop staring at me you damn bastard!'

HE KUPU IRAKORE — GENDER NEUTRALITY

When compared with English, but in truth, when compared to many other languages, te reo Māori uses a plethora of gender-neutral terms. Unlike languages that have an innate androcentricity woven into them reflecting the attitude of a time when women were chattels to be transferred from one man to another, te reo doesn't have these concepts. It is, for instance, impossible in Māori to say the phrase: 'Tahiti and her beautiful islands' because the third person singular possessive 'her' in te reo 'tōna' has no gender attached to it. The same goes for a ship, boat or waka. It has no gender so it is impossible to say something like 'She has a sturdy keel.' The irony is especially prevalent in famous book titles like *The Māori as He Was* written by Elsdon Best or J. Prytz-Johansen's *The Māori and His Religion*.

The word 'tāngata' is 'people', not 'men' so the well-known saying 'He whakaaro pai ki ngā tāngata katoa' is 'Goodwill to all people' in te reo not 'Goodwill to all men'. The word 'rangatira' or 'chief' has no gender associated with it. It is formed from a combination of 'rāranga' (to weave) and tira (groups) so a chief or leader is someone who weaves (often disparate) groups together, unifying them in purpose. Exactly how many women rangatira, for instance, signed the Treaty of Waitangi may never be known because, as shown below, traditional Māori names are not based on the gender of the child.

Even the simple pronoun 'ia' for 'him' or 'her' has no gender. You literally have to know who you are talking about before a gender is assigned to it.

There are a lot of these types of examples. Unlike in English where the old double standard applies in which promiscuous men are often called 'studs' and promiscuous women are 'sluts', there is the word 'kairau' in te reo for both genders. Literally 'consumer of many'. There is no implied judgement on whether it is considered good for men and bad for women. It simply is what it is.

Anatomy, once again, makes it clear who is in charge. 'He's got balls of steel' is impossible in te reo Māori as is the even more ludicrous 'She's got balls of steel'. Instead, the word 'māia' might be used: 'Ka nui tōna māia' — 'His/ her courage is gargantuan.' As mentioned, because of the influence of English, this is changing. Now, it is possible to hear 'He raho kore ia' — 'He/she has no balls'. This is not a traditional Māori concept or saying. Emotions and aspects of the human condition like anger or industry were associated with the stomach as in pukuriri (angry — literally, anger coming from the stomach) and pukumahi (industriousness, again, coming from the stomach). More aligned to the notion of having 'guts' but always gender neutral and therefore applicable to either males or females.

In my opinion, one of the worst examples of the sometimes quite nefarious influence of English and its characteristic sexism is the common term for a woman's period or menstruation. If you were to ask the majority of Māori women today what the term in te reo was for that life-affirming power, the answer would undoubtedly be 'mate wahine' — 'women's illness'. This is not a true Māori term and smacks of a time when Pākehā men were waiting outside the maternity ward smoking cigars and patting themselves on the back for a job well done while their wives were going through labour. The word I heard from native speakers of Taranaki when I was young was 'pāheke', to slip, to flow. A practical word that describes the action of menses, of blood flow. There is no association with anything negative because it is only experienced by women. Again, it just states the reality. For a fascinating delve into other words and terms for menstruation and associated mana wahine in the times of our tūpuna, check out the book *Te Awa Atua: menstruation in the pre-colonial Māori World* by Ngāhuia Murphy.

NGĀ INGOA — NAMES

An interesting aspect of Māori names is that, for the most part, they are gender neutral. When there is a gender assigned to them it is because it is in memory of a previous ancestor or it is to commemorate an historical incident. It is not because the baby or child is a boy or a girl. In fact, this did not seem to influence names at all. Take, for example, this tupuna, Tāneroroa.

Turi = Rongorongo
|
Tāneroroa

Turi was the leader of the Aotea waka and his wife Rongorongo was a leader in her own right. They had a number of children. Among them was a daughter named Tāneroroa (Tāneroa in some narratives). Note the word 'Tāne' in the name. Tāne means 'male' and while it could be a reference to the atua of trees and forests Tāne Mahuta, this is also considered a male entity so it clearly didn't matter if a child was a boy or a girl. The name was based on historical context not gender. There are many other tūpuna names like this.

Now contrast that with names that are loan words from English:

Male	Female
Anaru (Andrew)	Ani (Ann)
Hone (John)	Hūhana (Susan)
Mātene (Martin)	Mere (Mary)

When these loan word names became popular, every Māori person could speak te reo fluently. The ancestors could never imagine a time when te reo would become threatened and also these new-sounding names were different and exotic. Names held mana so it became a trend to name children after royalty, hence, names like Eruera (Edward), Hōri (George) and Wikitōria (Victoria).

But so what, right? They are just names. What's the harm?

You have, no doubt, caught on to the pattern here. Language communicates thought and influences thought. The gradual erosion of traditional Māori thinking and conversion into a hybrid of English and te reo might be fine — as all languages change and adapt to new and different stimuli — if te reo was in a strong state, spoken by millions and able to adjust itself organically, from the speakers themselves. But this is not the case with vulnerable languages that are only spoken fluently by numbers of people counted in the hundreds of thousands and nowhere else in the world. Like the example of the schoolboys talking about 'bitches' and using misogynist language in te reo at their total immersion school, all the examples above (and many more) demonstrate a change from outside te reo itself.

TE REO AND THE WIDER CULTURE

Okay, I'm cheating a little here. I already know the answer to the question 'is te reo sexist?' As I mentioned in Chapter One I wrote my master's degree thesis on this very subject. I always suspected te reo to be non-sexist and, in fact, that it enhances mana wahine, but I wanted to prove it and I did so with a 50,000-word thesis written in te reo in Taranaki dialect, so I know that there are many more examples that I could call on here. The point is that te reo Māori is born of indigeneity where the world only works if the mana of both women and men is upheld. It may have had different expressions, but I believe, the authentic aronga Māori, the traditional Māori worldview, enjoyed a status of mana between women and men that was, at least, a lot closer, if not the same.

While I am not proposing that te ao Māori before colonisation was a utopian paradise of hand holding and singing 'Kumbaya', there is ample evidence and knowledge handed down to consider the question: 'Is te reo Māori sexist?' I hope that you, too, have come to the same conclusion as I have. That, in its pure form, and left to its own devices, the Māori language is not a language intrinsically sexist, but with the influence of English it may be heading down a similar route.

So, if the language isn't inherently sexist, what about the wider culture and tikanga practices? Surely, if te reo is quite embracing and enhancing of mana wahine, the culture and tikanga must also reflect this point of view?

The short answer for me, unsurprisingly, is no. But as I have, hopefully, made clear with the example of the language above, the influence of colonisation, of the Bible, of missionaries, of a steady impact of introduced thinking and the erosion and replacing of traditional thinking, makes the statement 'Te ao Māori is not sexist' hard to put into practice and articulate. But I think there are two salient pathways to doing this: decolonisation and indigenisation.

Ways to restore mana

DECOLONISATION

For much of the Pākehā world, what the first missionaries taught here in Aotearoa, what the Bible says, religion and belief in God in general is an old-world faith that has little to no place in the modern world of the internet and globalism. For much of te ao Māori, however, the traditional connection to the elements and tūpuna through whaka-papa is lost and has been replaced with religion. When many elders (and younger people) whaikōrero or karanga now, much of the beauty of historical and authentic kōrero has been replaced by religious rhetoric.

While Taranaki and a few other regions have, to a degree, retained their traditional spirituality, many iwi have not. The teachings of the missionaries and the Bible are quite prominent in many rohe, and they have come to replace Māori thinking and tikanga. I met a young native speaker once who was taught that it was a traditional Māori tikanga that, during sex, it was only appropriate for the male to be on top. This was literally taught to some iwi by the missionaries (hence the term the 'missionary position') upon seeing all sorts of sexual activity present in the pre-colonised Aotearoa and, indeed, throughout Polynesia. That was two hundred odd years ago, but the legacy of their teachings has remained and is still being touted as true tikanga.

The Bible was the first book to be translated into te reo Māori and, of course, this was taken around the country and used to preach to convert the masses in Māori language.

E nga wahine, kia ngohengohe ki a koutou tane ake, hei mea ki te Ariki — Wives, submit to your own husbands, as to the Lord. Ephesians 5

Me ako marie te wahine kia nui te ngohengohe — Let a woman learn in silence with all submission. 1 Timothy, Chapter 2

E kore hoki e tukua e ahau te wahine kia whakaako, kia neke ake ranei tana tikanga i ta te tane, engari me ata noho — And I do not permit a woman to teach or to have authority over a man, but to be in silence. (Also in) 1 Timothy, Chapter 2

If you take a spiritual people and replace their spirituality with an imposed religion, with its values reflected in the above quotes, how can sexism not enter into Māori worldviews?

Decolonisation is the education of Māori people to deconstruct history and the impacts of colonisation on our thinking processes and tikanga practices. It is simply making Māori people aware of the changes that have gone on for them, that they were born into and had no choice in accepting. With this knowledge, they can, at least, begin to make informed decisions about what parts of colonisation they wish to keep or not. Our tūpuna were pretty keen on some of the new technology that was brought here from overseas, and I, myself, am quite partial to Netflix and gaming so I'm not advocating throwing the useful babies out with the colonised bathwater. I am saying, though, that Māori should be informed about our shared history in this country so that they can be clear on what they are making choices about in te ao Māori.

INDIGENISATION

The second part of that equation is to strengthen the knowledge and practice base of te ao Māori. Much of what I have written in this book is not known, understood or practised by the majority of Māori people. That should not be the case. Māoritanga, te ao Māori, te reo, tikanga should all be accessible to Māori as of right. I see and hear in the media many people believing that we live in a bicultural society, or even a multicultural society. This is probably because of the increase in recognition of te ao

Māori, te reo and tikanga and Pasifika and other cultures in recent years. We may be heading in that general direction, but we certainly don't live in a bicultural or multicultural society.

Being bilingual means speaking two languages fluently. Being a bicultural society means that there are two distinct cultures of equal status, funding and promotion running the nation. That is clearly not the case currently. Don't get me wrong, I like seeing bilingual signs in some shops, being able to use te reo on some phone apps, seeing waka ama out on the moana, having Māori carvings and latticework in some local and national government buildings, but these things a bicultural society does not make. What a truly bicultural society in Aotearoa New Zealand would entail is for an entirely different book, but suffice to say, there is a long way to go.

If we actually did live in an authentic bicultural society, you probably wouldn't be reading this book because you would have the same level of knowledge about the Māori world as you do about the rest of society. And, yes, I would like to see Pākehā eventually be knowledgeable in and participate in te ao Māori fully one day, but Māori people need to be much stronger in our knowledge, language and tikanga first.

We have already seen the influence that English has had on the aspect of sexism in te reo and the continued influence on Māori worldviews. To indigenise is to re-educate us to a strength in te ao Māori. I would like to see more Māori women, for instance, speaking te reo fluently again and able to engage in karanga as our kuia used to do. Performing karanga for as long as is appropriate, saying what they need to say and what they want to say. This is the true whaikōrero for women. And I have heard some amazing, wonderful karanga that included all the elements of the male whaikōrero with little exception. Truly wondrous to behold.

I would like to see women with such knowledge and fluency again that they are able to do 'pao', an impromptu song performed 'off the cuff' on a relevant topic or issue. And I would like Māori to have hundreds of waiata tawhito to choose from to put a point across, to comment on a circumstance, to support or not. The waiata are often chosen and carried by women. Having hundreds to pick from allows the singers to express their opinion.

These are the ways of indigenisation and the answer to the encroaching sexism in te ao Māori. These are the mana-enhancing ways of our tūpuna and we need to reacquaint ourselves with them.

The power of being informed

So, all very well, but is there a place for Pākehā in all this? Again, it's probably no surprise that I think, yes, there is. I am an educator and have been for many years so I have seen the power there is in being informed, in not being ignorant to other ways of speaking, thinking, living and being. Much like the example of pepeha in Chapter 5, I have never come across a Pākehā or Tauiwi person that has objected to being encouraged to say a different pepeha from a Māori person when it is explained what the reasoning is behind it. However, I have certainly seen much grief from people when it is just expected of them without any explanation. In short, becoming more familiar with Māori ideas, knowledge, language and customs is a good start.

What I would also recommend is education around the true history of this country, warts and all. For most of my lifetime it has felt like there has been a reticence, a reserve, about learning the actual history of the colonisation of Aotearoa as if it was a can of worms that no one wanted to open. I think the time has come when there is enough of a groundswell of determination to really explore it. Who knows, it might bring us together more and progress us towards a better bicultural society. There may even be a 'Kumbaya' or two in our shared future.

In aid of this possible future, being better informed or educated about our shared history and possible future while having a better understanding of te ao Māori may assist when it comes to judging Māori ways and tikanga. I mentioned politicians commenting on aspects of te ao Māori that they simply don't understand. This includes commenting on sensational incidents where powerful women in politics didn't get to speak at Waitangi and had to be seated behind the men for the pōwhiri.

Most marae have the mana and authority to determine who will speak, when and in what context. Women have spoken on the marae and continue to do so in some areas, though this is relatively uncommon. I believe that this is often due to the reality that the pōwhiri is a kawa ceremony that has to take place to manaaki manuhiri and lift the tapu of the guests and celebrate the kaupapa, in full cognisance that much of the decision making will be left to the rest of the hui and will be debated by all. Women are seated behind the men for the same reason that the Taranaki tikanga is that men go into the whare first during the pōwhiri. If there is conflict, though clearly not ideal, it is better that the men of your hapū or iwi are injured or killed. Without women, there is no hapū, iwi or future. These rituals of encounter have come from a time when that was possible and the community needs were paramount.

There is the whakataukī:

'He wahine, he whenua, e ngaro ai te tangata' —
'Through women and land are people lost'.

My interpretation of that is:

'Women and land are the only things worth giving your life for.'

That doesn't sound sexist to my taringa (ears). It sounds like a celebration of women's mana to me.

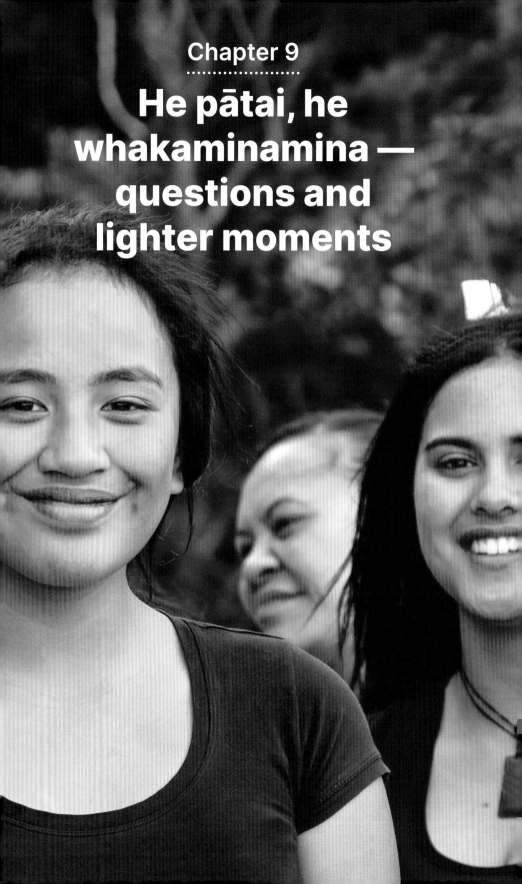

He pātai, he whakaminamina — questions and lighter moments

IN THIS FINAL CHAPTER I want to answer some of the questions that came up as a direct result of telling Pākehā and Tauiwi friends and colleagues that I was thinking of writing a book and asking them what sort of things that they have wondered about in te ao Māori. And then I would like to finish off with some lighter moments and memories that never fail to make me smile.

I dare to say, at this juncture, dear reader, you are starting to see that my opening statement at the beginning of this book is true. The Māori world is, indeed, a Māori universe.

A well-known whakataukī regarding education states:

'Ko te manu kai i te miro, nōna te ngahere. Ko te manu kai i te mātauranga, nōna te ao' — 'The bird that consumes the miro berry, the forest belongs to them. The bird that consumes knowledge, the entire world belongs to them.'

I would add to that:

'Ko te manu kai i te mātauranga Māori, mōna te ao tukupū' — 'The bird that consumes Māori knowledge, indigenous knowledge, for them, a boundless universe awaits.'

Some common queries

KAUMĀTUA

What exactly is a kaumātua? How does one become one? Is it dependent on age?

Leading means different things to different people/iwi/rohe, but people who 'do' are respected more. One of the realities that some regions have to deal with is the fact that there are not many people to do the tremendous amount of work within te ao Māori. Taranaki is one of these areas where there aren't that many people to uphold tikanga and te reo. It is increasing slowly in Taranaki, but it is an uphill battle. Many of us who are highly involved in things Māori have to do many jobs that would be associated with the role of kaumātua.

So, is this title given or taken because of age? At the time of writing my father is in his eighties, but he would not call himself a kaumātua (notwithstanding the fact that he still plays competitive table tennis and can beat me on most games on PlayStation). This is because he, like many Māori people, believe being called a 'kaumātua' is much more than about getting on in years. As with most things, there are iwi variations, but the etymology of the word was explained to me in this way:

He <u>matua</u> kua noho <u>kau</u>

A person of parent age (not a child or teenager) that has merely to sit, to dwell.

In other words, if you desire knowledge, you must seek out these people and go to them. They have earned their time to rest and are the wellsprings of knowledge, experience and wisdom. So, yes, clearly experience and wisdom are meant to come with age but, according to this definition, you are a kaumātua when your iwi and community say you are. It is not just a title one should take, but it is really an acknowledgement by the people who respect and support you that you have reached the status of learned elder.

Is it possible to be a thirty-year-old kaumātua? Well, yes, if your iwi and community back you because they are the ones who will have to defend this position if there is any grief given from other iwi or kaumātua. Most iwi, though, respect boundaries and believe that it is up to each iwi and rohe to 'appoint' their own kaumātua without judgement or interference from outside.

I have met a few of these rare individuals who were considered 'young kaumātua' and their knowledge in things Māori was truly impressive. But so was their standing with their communities. Without exception these kaumātua lived and breathed their Māoritanga and had spent years learning the different aspects of the marae. They had learnt from the back, starting with food preparation, digging both hāngī (earth ovens) and graves, preparing the wharenui, cleaning the toilets and all the mahi that is required to be seen as someone to depend on. A real 'ringa raupā' (an industrious worker with calloused hands). Only then were they taught the front part of the marae: the paepae, whaikōrero, karanga, karakia, and waiata tawhito. In the eyes of their kaumātua and teachers, they had earned a place to be taught and to hold the mana of the iwi even though they were relatively young.

Some people have even tried to adhere the label 'kaumātua' to me but, like my father, I just say, 'Give me another twenty or thirty years and I'll think about it.'

In recent years, the majority of native speakers of te reo and many of those who were taught at the feet of traditional experts of te ao Māori have passed away. Programmes and courses have become available to teach younger people the language and protocol of the marae that, in the past, would only be left to our elders because of their maturity, experience and wisdom. I understand this and I applaud the intention to train people up to carry the burden of te reo and tikanga on our marae, especially those marae that have little to no speakers left, but I urge caution.

I have encountered many of these 'young guns', and while they look and sound impressive, there is a dearth of depth, a lack of maturity and, worst of all, a serious absence of humility. Sometimes, being a good kaikōrero or kaikaranga means moving over or out of the way altogether when there is someone present who is more appropriate to kōrero or karanga, even if their language doesn't scale the heights of Ranginui. More and more, I'm seeing tauheke and kuia, who have spent their whole lives on the marae, getting pushed to the back so that people in their twenties can prance and peacock their way through karanga and whaikōrero.

When possible, I have challenged this. One taiohi told me that I should come to his course on Māoritanga because I might learn something. I told him I was quite happy with the thirty-five-year apprenticeship I had served. Another young man quoted a whakataukī about a bird to me. It was a pretty whakataukī. When I asked what the bird looked like, he made an excuse and left. He could parrot (no pun intended) quotes and sayings very well, but he had no practical experience with what he was talking about. I wasn't trying to embarrass him; I was just insinuating that it was best to have some real-world experience to go with rote-learned quotations. Another time my patience was wearing thin one day when a boasting youth told me how he had recently spoken at a major hui in front of thousands and he wished that I was there to listen to him. I had had quite enough of his conceit at this stage so I told him that when he had cleaned as many toilets on as many marae as I had, only then would I listen to what he had to say.

This is not just an older guy yelling at the sky, jealous of the injustice of not being youthful any more. This is the voice of experience over a long career encouraging younger people to be patient and humble. To take up the reins of leadership when their backs have earned the tokotoko (walking stick) that they are carrying, not because it looks cool and enhances the performance but because they need it from the years of bearing the load of responsibility.

Being Māori and indigenous

ARE THERE ANY FULL-BLOODED MĀORI PEOPLE LEFT?

Apart from being an offensive question because the inference is that having less than 100 per cent Māori blood makes you less Māori somehow, the answer is most definitely, yes. DNA tests that are relatively easy to get have shown some Māori to not have any other ethnicities in their genetic make-up, and there are some people who know their whakapapa inside out and can quite clearly show their lineage has no non-Māori DNA in it. One of my kaumātua who taught me used to say to me, 'When people ask if there are any full-blooded Māori people left, I want you to remember me. Only tūpuna Māori are in my blood.' His whānau carries on his legacy.

When (inevitably) Pākehā or Tauiwi people tell me 'You're not a full-blooded Māori', I say: 'Yes, of course I am. I'm a Māori full of blood!'

I BELIEVE I HAVE A MĀORI HEART. CAN I CLAIM TO BE MĀORI?

Not really, as being Māori is about whakapapa. If you have whakapapa Māori you belong to an iwi, hapū or whānau. I have met some pretty pale Māori people in my time so it is not about skin colour or whether you speak te reo; it is about whakapapa, and I have encouraged many people who did not grow up with their Māoritanga or even know much about it to pursue their roots. Some of the palest Māori I know are strong supporters of their marae, whānau, hapū or iwi. No one ever questions their whakapapa because they are there at tangi, hui, committee meetings, working bees and the like doing the hard yards. This is what is required to be accepted as part of the whānau. Funny how everyone is recognised as whānau at the marae with a tea towel or a paint brush in their hands.

MY FAMILY HAS BEEN IN NEW ZEALAND FOR FOUR GENERATIONS. WHEN DO I BECOME INDIGENOUS?

Sorry folks. Being indigenous is about, not coincidentally, indigeneity. When our Polynesian tūpuna arrived on these shores about one thousand years ago, there were no other people present. Māori people and culture flourished here, transforming from a seafaring Pacific people to tangata whenua, people of the land. If you are not Māori, you are here via the Treaty of Waitangi so, while you cannot be tangata whenua, you are instead, tangata tiriti.

MĀORI KING

Is there a Māori king? Yes, there is. (And there has been a queen, the late Te Arikinui Dame Te Atairangikaahu.) At the time of writing, he is Kīngi Tūheitia Pōtatau te Wherowhero te Tuawhitu. The Kīngitanga (Māori King Movement) was founded in 1858 with the aim of uniting iwi under a single leader, and by creating a monarch, being able to deal with Pākehā on equal footing, especially in the face of rampant land alienation. While many iwi around the motu support the kaupapa of the Kīngitanga, its main sphere of influence is in the Waikato, hence the nickname 'the King Country'.

Hei ngahau — some light moments

Within te ao Māori sometimes there is an impetus to make the most of good times because you know that the next time you see each other, it might be for a sad occasion. There is something magical about being with friends and whānau, playing the guitar, singing up a storm and relishing the time you have together. Some of my favourite times in experiencing the Māori universe have been when I've enjoyed good company and a good laugh. With this in mind, I thought it might be entertaining to share some of the lighter moments and downright hilarious situations that I've experienced.

TE REO LEARNERS

As usual, I'll begin with some te reo use. As much as I want to support people in their learning of te reo Māori, as a fluent speaker, it is sometimes very difficult, and sometimes absolutely impossible, to not laugh at mistakes made. Now, that sounds mean, but read on and think about how you would have reacted.

As a teacher of Māori language, I have had to take many students through their assessments. Basically, they are tests that give a good picture of where the learner is at, with pronunciation, vocab and so on. One such student assessment was going well until it came time for the young woman to recite a karakia. Without knowing, she inserted the famous 'Hakuna Matata' phrase from the movie *The Lion King* into her karakia. It went like this: 'Tēnei au e noho hakuna matata nei'. This was side-splitting for me, but she was so nervous that I had to hold my tongue and laughter until she had gotten through all the other content and left the room lest I put her off the rest of her assessment.

And speaking of mixing up words in te reo, I was sitting at the dinner table on the marae one time when a learner sat opposite me. Her fluency was coming along, but often students get nervous in front of their tutors, and this is what happened in this case. She said to me: 'Kei te pīrangi au ki te mitimiti i ō kēkē.' I said, 'I think you mean "keke" [cake].' As we have seen, long vowels (indicated by macrons in written language) make all the difference, changing the word entirely. She had said in Māori 'I want to lick your armpits.' Unfortunately, she followed this up with: 'Homai te toto' — 'Pass me the blood.' She meant 'tote' — salt.

I'm not sure if it is just the nature of some politicians, but here is yet another example of a Pākehā politician trying to run before they can walk when it comes to te reo. He insisted on delivering a large proportion of his speech in te reo. Most of it was too mangled to make heads or tails of, but he did manage to clearly start with an inappropriate tauparapara (which, you'll remember from Chapter 4 is a component of the traditional whaikōrero). This politician belted out a tauparapara that had nothing to do with the kaupapa of his speech in the first place, was only done by him to show off in the second place and got it completely wrong in the third place. He shouted:

Ka tangi te titi!
Ka tangi te kaka!

While kaka isn't a Māori word for excrement, it is so widely known as a slang term for it that te reo speakers in the audience couldn't help but laugh out loud. He had just shouted:

My tit cries!
My shit cries!

On the plus side, it did rhyme …

BURDENS

Part of any apprenticeship involves long hours of learning, of repetition, of practice and gaining experience. I have been responsible for the tikanga of the paepae many times, but there was one instance that proved to be a turning point in my willingness to forfeit my own health and well-being to make sure that the tikanga ran smoothly on the marae.

As I have mentioned several times, there are some regions and some marae with very few people to uphold the mana of the reo and tikanga of the paepae. On one occasion, I was put solely in charge of running every tikanga aspect at a tangihanga. There simply were no other people to do the karakia, the whaikōrero, or even the waiata. For three days I held the paepae entirely on my own. I would start at 7 am and finish at around 10 pm. Every single manuhiri that arrived was given a mihi so I was averaging twenty-five to thirty whaikōrero per day. I wasn't able to have a meal or even drink a full cup of tea as the manuhiri kept coming in droves. I was running on empty by the third day with little sleep and less nourishment. When there seemed to be a small break in the avalanche of manuhiri, I quickly scuttled off to the toilet. Within two minutes someone was knocking on the cubicle door screaming, 'We've got more manuhiri!' Toilet paper in hand I bellowed back, 'Well, tell them to bloody wait because I'm damn well busy!'

That proved to be the metaphorical straw that broke the camel's back and I vowed to look after my own time, energy and health better so that I could live a long life and contribute more to my community and te ao Māori.

RAP AND RADIO

A kuia once told me that te reo Māori was an ancient language that only had its place in ceremonies on the marae. It wasn't for modern times or for use on radio, TV or computers. I said to her, 'With respect, e Kui, I don't believe that. And I'll prove it to you!' And that was how the first rap in te reo Māori was born. The first line was 'Kaua e āwangawanga, e hoa mā, e kore tō tātou reo e ngaro rawa!' — Yes, it even rhymes. This first line means 'Don't worry, friends, our precious language will never be lost.' It was a mild hit on Māori radio, and one of my best memories is rapping in Māori to an audience of hundreds with the band Upper Hutt Posse. I went on to be a broadcaster on

Te Korimako o Taranaki, the Taranaki iwi radio where I created comedy and drama shows all in te reo. That was such fun! And I think I proved my point that te reo Māori was as modern and as adaptable as any other language in the world.

THE 'ENTERTAINER'

As I've said, I grew up quite poor and had little money for koha. When a group from the marae were going to a hui in Rūātoki, deep within the heart of Ngāi Tūhoe, I once again realised that I was without funds for a koha. In the impetuousness of youth, I decided that seeing as though I had no money, my koha would be to try, at least, to entertain the tangata whenua. Rūātoki was then and is still now one of the few communities where te reo is the dominant language among the permanent residents. I was amazed to see the paepae stacked with at least ten native speakers and no one was under eighty years old. To this day, Tūhoe are one of the staunchest iwi when it comes to their Māoritanga.

That night, after karakia, we were introducing ourselves and I hatched my cunning plan to 'entertain'. I stood up and after the appropriate mihi and pepeha I divulged that I had secretly stowed away so that I could find a Tūhoe wife, and I asked if anyone was interested in taking up my offer. As it turns out, there was plenty of interest. Kuia after kuia, with no teeth and, again, no one under eighty, all got up and said how they had been widowed years ago and would love the opportunity to teach this young pup some new tricks ...

Very fortunately for me, my kaumātua stood up and told everyone that disappointingly I was in a taumou (betrothed) situation back home in Taranaki and that while I was unhappy with this arrangement, I had to see it through for the mana of my hapū.

Later, my kaumātua told me very clearly not to ever do that again or he wouldn't bail me out the next time.

HARD-NOSED

Dawn kawa ceremonies are a mainstay for those of us immersed in te ao Māori and heavily involved in the revitalisation of more traditional practices. Usually, whare are opened at dawn, but in the modern age with city and town councils wanting to try to be more respectful of Māori customs, many events and exhibitions are opened with Māori ceremonies. At one such dawn ceremony for the opening of a new Māori exhibition at an art gallery, the kaumātua and I, followed by about fifty others, went around the exhibition reciting our karakia.

It was just before dawn and so it was almost impossible to see anything. No one had thought to bring a torch so that we could, at least, know where we were going. We fumbled our way around in the dark, encountering a man standing in our way. In the circumstances it would have been rude not to hongi him and so we all did so. It seemed strange, but we thought perhaps he had just gone the wrong way in the dark and we were focused on our karakia and the ceremony so we carried on.

It wasn't until the ceremony was over that we turned on the lights to see that fifty people had pressed noses with one of the mannequins in the exhibition. No wonder his nose had felt quite rigid . . .

BURSTING THE FORMAL BUBBLE

Kawa ceremonies are taken very seriously and are some of the most tapu events I have ever been to and led. When I am the kaikarakia (ceremonial leader) I have a whole ritual of my own that I go through to prepare for such a tapu undertaking. Unfortunately, it's a bit like the seriousness and formality of many a church service in that if something funny happens and you start laughing, it is nearly impossible to stop.

I was merely a participant in one dawn opening when during this most tapu of ceremonies, a person started singing at the top of their lungs with a voice whose shrieks would drown out the entire New Zealand Symphony Orchestra if every instrument was out of tune.

And the person's choice of traditional waiata Māori to enhance the sanctity of the kawa ceremony? A Rod Stewart ballad — if Rod had his feet on fire and was trying to put them out by screaming at them.

Folks, I usually pride myself on being able to just be in the moment when it comes to Māori things, but the sights and sounds that engulfed my focus on that day had me, quite literally, rolling on the floor laughing. Gleeful tears streamed down my face in recognition of the hilarity of the situation. And, though people were loath to admit it later, I was not the only one.

This is the reality of the human experience. The best laid plans can go awry, and they certainly did that day.

Remarkably, the kaumātua who carried the karakia and ceremony of the day remained focused and completed the task at hand without the slightest hint of pause. That pure force of will in the face of such distraction is to be praised and admired.

He whakakapinga — to conclude

If the Māori world is a Māori universe, I hope you have enjoyed at least exploring around our rocky planets in the immediate solar system. And I hope I have piqued your interest enough to consider exploring further, beyond the gas giants, into the boundless Māori universe that awaits . . .

Tērā puanga ka rewa i te pae
Te tohu rā kua pahemo te tau o mua
Ko te tau hou kua tau mai nei
E mahara whakamua ana

(There rises Rigel yonder above the horizon
A sure sign that the Māori new year is upon us
Let me contemplate what has been
And the potential for all that yet may be)
— He whakahīnga nā Keri (an original composition, 1995)

Noho ora mai koutou, e aku kaipānui, i raro i te maru o Ranginui e tū nei, i roto hoki i te mahana o Papatūānuku e takoto nei — Remain in good health, dear readers, under the mantle of Rangi the sky father and within the warmth of the embrace of Papa the earth mother.

Kia ora mai rā

Mōku ake — about the author

KERI OPAI is a linguist, educator and the author of *Te Reo Hapai*, the seminal work in creating a Māori language glossary for mental health, disability and addiction. He gained a Māori interpreters licence at the age of twenty-one, and advises widely on cultural issues.